GW00566880

Balloon Tytler

by the same author

—

THE MAN BEHIND MACBETH:
AND OTHER STUDIES

Nº 119

BRITISH MUSEUM BANKS COLLECTION

C. 2 - 23

EDINBURGH FIRE BALLOON
By I. Tytler
Price 3 Shillings.

J. Tytler

The Grand Edinburgh Fire Balloon

Balloon Tytler

SIR JAMES FERGUSSON
OF KILKERRAN

FABER AND FABER LTD
3 Queen Square London

First published in 1972
by Faber and Faber Limited
3 Queen Square, London, WC1
Printed in Great Britain
by W & J Mackay Limited, Chatham
All rights reserved

ISBN 0 571 09986 6

© *Sir James Fergusson 1972*

To my son Adam

Acknowledgements

I record my grateful thanks to the staffs of the National Library of Scotland, the Scottish Record Office, the Signet Library, the Edinburgh Central Public Library, Edinburgh University Library and the Essex Institute, Salem, Massachusetts, for their courteous and ample help in my researches.

Contents

Illustrations

Outline of Tytler's life

17 Dec. 1745	Born at Fearn.
c.1761	Surgeon's apprentice in Forfar.
c.1764	Student at Edinburgh University.
1765	Surgeon in whaling ship.
27 Oct. 1765	Proclamation of marriage to Elizabeth Rattray.
c.1766	Goes to Northumberland.
1772	Returns to Edinburgh.
1774	First publications.
23 Feb. 1775	Enters debtors' sanctuary at Holyrood.
1776–84	Edits *Encyclopaedia Britannica*, 2nd ed.
1780	Begins *Weekly Mirror*.
25 Aug. 1784	Balloon 'fairly floated'.
27 Aug. 1784	First balloon ascent.
31 Aug. 1784	Second balloon ascent.
18 Mar. 1785	Again enters debtors' sanctuary.
23 Jan. 1788	Elizabeth Rattray begins process of divorce.
3 Mar. 1788	Tytler in Berwick.
July 1791	Begins *Historical Register*.
4 Dec. 1792	Arrested and finds caution.
7 Jan. 1793	Outlawed for non-appearance.
8 Aug. 1795	Lands at Salem, Mass.
1799	*Treatise on the Plague and Yellow Fever*.
31 July 1801	Agrees to compile *Universal Geography*.
9 Jan. 1804	Dies at Salem.

Introduction

The life of James Tytler, who was born in 1745 and died in 1804, was one of occasional notoriety but general obscurity. The former was just enough for him to be remembered by his contemporaries, the latter to make factual record of him very hard to find. He moved in the seedier part of Edinburgh society in the age of Boswell and Burns and did not catch the eye of its many annalists. His one striking achievement drew less attention than it deserved and was very soon almost forgotten. Yet it alone entitles him to remembrance. He was the first man in Great Britain to rise from its surface in a balloon —a balloon, moreover, which he had designed himself—and from that feat he became known, more in mockery than admiration, as 'Balloon Tytler'.

The balloon episode was however only one in a long career of remarkable variety. Tytler was in turn chemist, surgeon, printer, mechanic, journalist, editor, poet and pamphleteer. In every one of these callings he failed to reach success or profit. His life was one of poverty and disappointment, struggle and defeat. Yet he was learned, ingenious, active and versatile. Many men with fewer talents have raised themselves to comfort and reputation. Tytler seemed to be doomed to fail and moreover to fail ridiculously.

There have been a few short biographies or rather biographical sketches of Tytler, but all see him from a distance. In 1805, the year of his death, an anonymous writer, identified as one Robert Meek, published a short life of him, hastily written, cheaply and badly printed. Its content is meagre, concentrating on Tytler's literary work and mentioning the balloon flight very briefly and only as a failure. Meek wrote in admiration of Tytler's 'extraordinary talents' and his little book has some value for its early appearance and a few anecdotes gathered from some of Tytler's acquaintances, unfortunately without naming them. But since Meek never met Tytler himself his account lacks precision and detail and it touches only a few years of his life.

Next comes a sketch incorporated as a note of over four pages in Robert Cromek's *Reliques of Robert Burns*, published in 1808, and reprinted in 1810 in the same editor's *Select Scotish Songs*. It was the work, as Cromek acknowledged, of Dr Robert Anderson and though so short is the only authoritative contemporary account of Tytler's life. Anderson, who was five years younger than Tytler, had a curiously parallel career in which he found the success as a man of letters that eluded the other. Like Tytler he began life as a surgeon, practising in Northumberland, but settled in Edinburgh in 1784, the very year of Tytler's balloon ascents. Like Tytler he turned to literature, and in particular to editing the work of other men, but did it with a competence that earned him a living and a respectable standing. He even wrote lives of Johnson and Smollett which reached a third and fourth edition respectively. Like Tytler he edited a magazine; but whereas Tytler's editorial ventures invariably collapsed Anderson's *Edinburgh Magazine* flourished for nine years till it was incorporated with the long established *Scots Magazine*. Travelling smoothly on the high road of literature while Tytler floundered in its byways, and living in Edinburgh through several years of Tytler's life there, Anderson is an excellent witness. He certainly knew Tytler well, even with some intimacy, and his own character was upright and truthful.

Meek and Anderson supplied some of the materials for James Paterson, who wrote an account of Tytler to go with John Kay's caricature 'Fowls of a Feather Flock Together', showing five figures of whom Tytler is one. Kay was an Edinburgh barber with a talent for lifelike caricature. He died in 1826 and a collection of his prints was published in 1837–8 (re-issued in 1877). The accompanying letterpress was begun by James Maidment, an advocate, but most of the work of gathering the information and writing the biographical sketches was done by James Paterson, who patiently hunted through old newspaper files and also tracked down 'several old and communicative individuals' in search of anecdotes. Paterson was an experienced and conscientious Ayrshire journalist with a bent for history. His account of Tytler, based on notes left by Kay, is valuable, but it contains some inaccuracies and was written over 30 years after Tytler's death.

Last of these sketches of Tytler's life comes the long entry in the *Biographical Dictionary of Eminent Scotsmen* published in 1847 by Robert Chambers, the author of *Traditions of Edinburgh*. This adds very little fact though much moralizing to the former accounts and regarding the balloon experiments is extremely incorrect.

Tytler's only fragment of autobiography is an account of his balloon venture added to a congratulatory poem which he addressed to the much more successful balloonist Vincent Lunardi. This appeared in 1786 in Lunardi's book *An Account of Five Aerial Voyages in Scotland*. It has to be read with reserve but is at least first-hand.

This total of information from Meek, Anderson, Chambers and Tytler himself is somewhat meagre, but it is no more than a first survey of the field. A second and more thorough one amplifies and often corrects the first. Hardly anyone who lived in eighteenth-century Scotland or America left no trace of his sojourn in this world, and most people left many, the milestones, if no more, of their passage. Tytler was no exception. Some major events of his life—his birth and parentage, his marriage and its breakdown, his frequent financial troubles, his brushes with the law—left their predictable entries in the public records. Occasionally, especially during his short notoriety as a balloonist, the newspapers took note of him.

Once he was the subject of correspondence between men in high places. Moreover, since he was a prolific writer, his own publications mark some of his footsteps and reveal his purposeful, if erratic, progress through life. What is strange is the disappearance of almost all his letters, though a man with so ready a pen must have written hundreds. Probably no one thought them worth keeping.

So, after patient search and piecing evidence together, Tytler emerges from the shadows, often a little misty himself but sometimes caught in a ray of clear light. It becomes understandable why his biographers saw him as one rather to be pitied for his misfortunes than blamed for his faults: a busy, hopeful, wandering, shabby figure, too petty to be tragic, too earnest to be comic, searching tirelessly for success and recognition and never finding them, one of the poor waifs of history.

I

Early Years

The parish of Fearn where Tytler was born in 1745 was a remote and backward district of Angus—or Forfarshire, as it was then called—which sloped from high hills, abounding with grouse and blackgame, down towards the south-east, 'a very fyne brae countrey', as an old writer described it. Much of the soil was good, but on the small farms which made up the parish the age of the improvers had not yet dawned. An area of some 20 square miles contained a population of about 500 people which was beginning to dwindle and continued to do so for the rest of the century and later.

The countryside looked empty. There were hardly any trees except a few planes and ashes set round the modest vegetable gardens ('yards') beside the squalid little farm-houses with their thatched roofs and earth floors. Nearly everyone in the parish won his living from the soil. There were a few essential craftsmen—tailors, weavers, shoemakers, and a smith—but Fearn did not contain a village. No turnpike road ran through the parish, whose only link with the outside world was the rough hilly road to Brechin, seven miles away. Even a hundred years later a minister of Fearn could write: 'The only places of common resort are the parish church and school. We have no tavern, no news-room, no lodge, no club, and no special association, civil, social, or religious, which we can call our own.'

To the little manse, near the old church which was to be rebuilt 60 years later, Mr George Tytler brought his wife Janet Robertson and his family in the early spring of 1745. The Presbytery of Brechin admitted him to the charge of Fearn on 24 April. He was 39 years old and had been minister of Premnay in Aberdeenshire since 1733. Married a year after his first induction, he and his wife already had three children. Their fourth, James, was born on the 17th of the following December, the day on which the Highland army which had startled the kingdom in the autumn reached Shap on its retreat from England. Another son, Henry, was born more than seven years later. Other children who did not survive were perhaps born in the interval.

In these quiet and rural surroundings James passed his childhood. He is said to have received an excellent education. Its foundation was no doubt laid in the parish school which stood close to the church, but most of it he owed to his father, who was a graduate of Marischal College, Aberdeen, and taught his three sons Latin and Greek. The eldest boy, George, was destined for the ministry. He became a divinity student but nothing more is known of him except that he went abroad. Henry, the youngest, ultimately became a doctor and must have been a good Greek scholar, for he was remembered for having published a translation of the poems of Callimachus. As Mr Tytler's stipend was only 1000 merks Scots, equivalent to £55 sterling, and moreover paid not in cash but 'in victual', obviously the maintenance of his eldest son at a university would be as much as he could be expected to afford. James would have to fend for himself.

This he seemed quite able to do. From his earliest years he read 'with avidity' every book that fell in his way, and he had an excellent memory. His father gave him 'an extensive acquaintance with biblical literature and scholastic theology' besides the classics. He is said to have acquired very early a great fund of general knowledge, particularly of history, and he must also have read what books of science he could find. But his reading, apart from the theology inculcated by his father, was probably as unplanned and undisciplined as it was wide.

He claimed in his later years to have studied at Aberdeen but to have left it at the age of 15. It was alleged to Meek after his death that his father dissuaded him from trying to enter the ministry. It seems likelier that he had no inclination to it. His father apprenticed him at an early age, probably in 1761, to a surgeon in Forfar named Ogilvie. His work there was probably no more than to prepare the drugs used by his master and to deliver them and other messages, but at least it confirmed his bent for medicine and gave him some rudimentary knowledge of chemistry. His wages, if any, must have been very small but at least his master would give him board and lodging so that he was no burden to the family at Fearn manse. From there Forfar was only nine miles distant; but if James was to get on in the world he must move further away.

There is no means of knowing how the decision was taken and the necessary funds scraped together, but after a year or two with Mr Ogilvie, James went to Edinburgh and began to attend the medical classes at the University. He exchanged the braes of Angus and their pure fresh winds, their open fields and scattered farms, for the narrow confines, the smoke and the stenches of a busy and crowded city. For the first time he trod those steep, filthy streets among which he was to pass a great part of his life.

Edinburgh was still substantially the old town rebuilt in the 16th century after the devastation of the English wars. High and close-packed it clustered on its rocky ridge between the great castle brooding above it and, beyond the Canongate that continued the line of the High Street, the low-lying palace of Holyroodhouse. The palace, once splendid but now neglected, which had not been a royal residence for 80 years, served a number of purposes. Some of its large apartments were used as public halls—for the elections of the Scottish representative peers, for meetings of other bodies, or for important social events like the Hunters' Ball. Suites of smaller rooms were occupied as private flats by various noble families. The western face of the stately building was obscured by a huddle of houses massed within the Sanctuary, that precinct, including the

King's Park to the south and a good extent of other ground in the palace's vicinity, which was administered by the Bailie of Holyrood and outside the jurisdiction of the Edinburgh magistrates. Within the Sanctuary debtors could live secure from arrest until they could discharge their obligations. This was a part of Edinburgh that Tytler was to come to know well.

The mile-long street leading down from the castle, the only one in Edinburgh of real breadth, was interrupted at three points: first by the massive Tolbooth—partly a council chamber and partly a prison—and the narrow pile of houses and shops that all but blocked it on the north side of the High Kirk: next by the City Guardhouse which stood in the middle of it some 200 yards below the mercat cross; and lower down by the building known as the Netherbow Port which spanned its final stretch and gave access to the Canongate. The Port, crowned with a tower and spire, had a gateway in the middle for wheeled vehicles and a small wicket beside it for pedestrians. But increasing traffic was too much for it, the building was too 'crazy' for the gateway to be enlarged, and so in August 1764 the Netherbow Port was pulled down. James Tytler came to Edinburgh just in time to see the last of this ancient landmark. Another famous Edinburgh gate, the venerable Foir Yett leading to the palace, had been destroyed, with much less reason, a few years before.

On either side of the High Street and the Canongate towered the 'lands', six, seven or more storeys high, pierced by narrow closes leading inwards to other dwellings in the courts and alleys behind. Tradesmen and craftsmen occupied the lowest floors of these lofty buildings; gentry, lawyers and rich merchants the middle ones; aristocratic and often eccentric old ladies living on tiny annuities the upper flats; and the poorest inhabitants were massed in the garrets. It would be among the latter that a poor student like Tytler would find himself some sort of lodging. In the cellars flourished a rich social life among taverns and eating-houses where met the numerous clubs to which many of the most eminent citizens belonged.

More important to Tytler were the handsome new Royal Infirmary erected in 1738 and the cranky, crowded buildings of the University opposite to it where he began his real study of medicine. He could have taken no better step towards his projected career, for the University at this time boasted three great teachers, William Cullen, the professor of chemistry, Alexander Monro, the professor of anatomy, and John Rutherford, the professor of medicine.

Rutherford, the oldest of the three, had inaugurated the practice, in which Cullen followed him, of giving clinical lectures at the Royal Infirmary. He lectured always in Latin, which language he was said to know better than his own. Cullen used Latin in his botanical lectures, but otherwise both he and Monro lectured in English.

Dr Alexander Monro *secundus* was one of the great trio of Monros —father, son and grandson—who between them filled the chair of anatomy at Edinburgh for over a century. He spoke with slow formality and his lectures usually lasted for over an hour, but they were impressive and memorable and he was most earnest in discharging the duties of his chair.

But the professor from whom James must have learnt most was Cullen, who during the young man's time at the University still held the chair of chemistry but moved from it in 1766 to that of medicine in succession to Rutherford. He was a well-known figure in the city, tall, thin and stooping, with an abstracted air as he passed along the streets. This man was the real originator of the study of scientific chemistry in Great Britain. As one of his pupils quaintly wrote: 'Chemistry, which was before his time a most disgusting pursuit, was by him rendered a study so pleasing, so easy, and so attractive, that it is now prosecuted by numbers as an agreeable recreation.' According to another, 'he was the first person in this country who made chemistry cease to be a chaos'.

Cullen, who had a most retentive memory, lectured without notes, and one aspect of his brilliance was his power to raise not merely interest but enthusiasm among his students. His lectures were crowded. Moreover he went out of his way to show his students as individuals every sort of kindness, inviting them by twos and threes to supper till he had made the acquaintance of his whole class. He lent them books from his library and helped them in all their difficulties. 'They seemed to be his family.' He knew them all so well that he was aware of their financial difficulties, and his benevolence towards the really poor students was both active and tactful. To them he was most insistent in lending books, and he even, in the most delicate way, devised means of dodging acceptance of the fees due to him from them.

It must have been Cullen's teaching that inspired James Tytler while a student at Edinburgh to take up experimental chemistry, the interest to which he turned at various periods of his life and which under a happier star he might have pursued as his profession. Cullen's generosity towards his poorer students offers, too, a possible explanation of how Tytler was able to study at Edinburgh at all in spite of his father's modest means. But neither that nor the occasional bag of oatmeal sent from Fearn could altogether support him in however frugal a way of living. He had to find some vacation employment, and in doing so he showed a spirit of adventure and resourcefulness, turning to advantage his still limited knowledge of medicine. In the spring of 1765, at the age of 19, he took service as surgeon aboard a whaling-ship bound for the Greenland seas.

Meek, the earliest of Tytler's biographers, states positively that 'he made two voyages to Greenland during the vacation', but in fact he made only one, in 1765. Some details of this adventurous interlude can be gathered, although the history of the Scottish whale fishery in the 18th century has yet to be written. The bare framework of it is extant among the records of the Scottish Exchequer, but these can only hint at extraordinary tales of arduous and perilous enterprise. The largest of the whale-ships sailing from Scottish ports at this time, the *Dundee*, was of only 351 tons, and most were far smaller: the *North Star*, of Dunbar, was of only 236. Yet these were fair-sized sea-going vessels for the time. The *Dundee's* 351 tons may be compared with the 366 tons of Captain Cook's *Endeavour*.

The ships put to sea usually in April, seldom as early as March, and generally returned in July or August, though sometimes, if they had been unfortunate in their search for whales, not till September. Before sailing each skipper obtained a licence from the Commissioner of Customs at Leith after he and the mate had taken an oath that whaling and whaling alone was the purpose of their voyage. On the ship's return her catch was registered at the Leith Custom House and a bounty of 40s per ton of the ship's displacement was then paid.

A good cargo was the blubber of two or more whales. The *Campbeltown* of Leith, 303 tons, sailed on 13 April 1770 and returned on 9 August with 113 casks filled with the blubber of three whales. That was an excellent catch. But in the same season the *Peggy* of Glasgow, 238 tons, returned a week later with no more than the blubber of six seals filling but a single cask, and in the following year she came home at the end of the season with no catch at all. 'A clean ship' or 'Nothing but empty casks' are phrases coldly recording long weeks of hardship and danger in the Arctic seas with no reward but disappointment, though the bounty was paid as usual.

The ships were either British built or 'British plantation built' and the crews were mostly British but often included a few foreigners who had to be declared as such when the bounty was granted. They were divided into 'harpooners', 'steersmen', 'line-managers' and apprentices, the last being indentured for three years or more. The captain and the mate were the only officers but each ship carried a surgeon: broken or sprained limbs, digestive troubles from bad food and sea sores of all kinds must have been the common lot of the seamen. Every whaler's surgeon may not have been so scantily qualified as James Tytler but each must have gained plenty of experience by the time his ship regained the port of Leith.

Tytler's ship was the *Royal Bounty* of Leith, British plantation built, of 331 tons burthen, William Ker master. She carried six boats, a crew of 36 seamen and six apprentices. Six of the men were foreigners—Dutch, to judge by their names. The date of the *Royal Bounty*'s sailing is lost but she came into Leith on 13 August 1765 after a voyage of only moderate success. On board were 33 casks containing the blubber and 'cring' of only one whale 'and the fins thereof'. The following year, when the skipper was one James Boyd and the surgeon William Proctor, she returned empty. But she made a much better voyage in 1770, under yet another skipper, bringing home the blubber of four whales in 174 casks.

Many years later Tytler wrote two accounts of the whale fishery which are of real value since so little was ever written of it from direct experience. It appears that his voyage in the *Royal Bounty* was not towards Greenland but to the seas around Spitzbergen, but conditions throughout the northern fishery were no doubt alike. Each of the whaling ship's boats carried six men. As soon as the ship had reached suitable waters two boats, moored to pieces of floating ice, were kept constantly on the watch for whales, and were relieved by other boats every four hours. If a whale was sighted both boats set off in pursuit, and if they were fortunate enough to overtake him one of the harpooners lodged a harpoon in his side. Immediately an oar would be set upright in the boat as a signal to the ship, aboard which the look-out would hail the deck with 'Fall! Fall!' The other boats then put off to the assistance of the first two.

The rope fastened to the harpoon was of 200 fathoms, carefully coiled to run out steadily as the wounded whale made off, at first 'with prodigious violence'. The rope would run out at such a speed that there was danger that its friction would set fire to the gunwale, which would be wetted to prevent it. If the whale was strong and not badly hurt he would take out the whole line, and the seamen would have to be alert to bend on to it the line from the next boat, and if necessary the next if it had joined them in time. A whale had been known to take more than 1000 fathoms of line before he tired, but whenever he did it was the duty of the 'line-managers' to haul in and re-coil the slackened line, heavy and dripping with icy seawater, until at length the pursuers could close with the whale and either attack him with fresh harpoons or wait for the last of his struggles until he finally expired, reddening the sea with his blood.

The ship meanwhile had been following the boats, and when the chase was ended the huge corpse would be lashed alongside her with two of the boats secured outside it to prevent accidents and the loss of men or tools. Three or four men, 'with irons at their feet to prevent slipping', then climbed down on to the whale and set to work to cut off pieces of blubber, eight feet long and three feet thick, which were hauled on board by capstan or windlass. The rest of the crew were employed in slicing up the blubber into smaller pieces, 'picking out the lean', and stowing them below decks. Finally the carcase was turned loose and if it was washed on to the ice was eagerly stripped of its flesh by the polar bears.

When the ship had captured as many whales as she could deal with, or by the end of August had to turn homewards, either laden or empty, so as to get clear of the ice, the blubber was cut up still smaller and packed into casks, 'cramming them very full and close'. Not till the ship reached port could it be boiled down into train-oil.

Such was the voyage of a whaler in those days. It must have been a rough life for a country boy, and a strange one—the cramped quarters, the coarse food, the fantastic drama of the whale-hunt, the stench of blood and blubber in the long, long, glittering Arctic days. James probably hated it. He never went to sea again for nearly thirty years.

Once more he trod the streets of Edinburgh. But the medical classes did not begin till November—and he was never to return to them.

2

Writing to Eat

James Tytler was not the first man nor the last to jeopardize his prospects by an imprudent early marriage, but in his case the damage to his career seems to have been total. He had to abandon study for a profession and begin at once to earn a living. The step let him into a permanent struggle against poverty in the effort to keep his wife and family, a series of shifts which never provided him with a regular or sufficient livelihood.

It must have been a hasty and impulsive marriage into which he entered at the end of October 1765, little more than two months after his return from sea. It followed on a time of some emotional disturbance. Perhaps after some dog-watch discussions of religion with one or more of his shipmates in the *Royal Bounty*, Tytler became involved, soon after he left her, with the small sect known as the Glasites. This body had been founded by an Angus minister, Mr John Glas, who in 1726 had caused a sensation by preaching against the Covenants and after publishing a book on his opinions had been deposed from the ministry in 1730.

The Glasites, who were also called Sandemanians after Mr Robert Sandeman, Glas's son-in-law, who took over the leadership of the movement, were a mild and gentle people, holding that religion should be based on love and expressed in voluntary association. The Covenants of 1638 and 1643, which had protested the inviolability of Presbyterian church government, the Glasites thought intolerant, and they had scruples about the connections of Church and State. The Church of Scotland, after many years of struggle,

had been established as Presbyterian in 1690 and its position as the
national Church confirmed by an Act of Parliament annexed to the
Act of Union in 1707. This establishment the Glasites, like some
other minorities, could not accept. They held that a national Church,
recognized and secured by the secular power, was not in accordance
with Scripture. Unlike most seceders, they did not profess to maintain the original purity of the body which they had quitted but
adopted customs of their own. These included a revival of the early
Christian love-feast or *agape*, which the Glasites celebrated with
broth.

Tytler's association with these eccentric but amiable people did
not last for more than a few months. Perhaps the love-feasts bored
him; perhaps his lapse from the Glasites was simply due, as Anderson
states, to 'an unsteadiness that was natural to him'. One of his later
writings certainly shows that he found their principles too rigid.
His brief membership of this fraternal sect does however suggest
that he had a sociable nature; and its cessation indicated no change
in him. He remained a Christian all his life, and, says Anderson, 'a
zealous advocate of genuine Christianity', but he never again became a member of any religious denomination. His versatile and
wandering life fitted into no conventional pattern of behaviour.

Brief though the association was, it was the cause of his marriage.
Among the Glasites of Edinburgh was a girl with whom he fell in
love. She was an orphan—Elizabeth Rattray, the daughter of a
deceased writer (i.e. solicitor) named James Rattray whose wife
had been one Anne Blair. In the proclamation of Elizabeth's forth-
coming marriage on Sunday 27 October her father was described as
having been 'writer in Edinburgh', but at the time of her action for
divorce twelve years later he was styled 'writer in Perth'. Since
Rattray is a Perthshire name his professional career may have lain
formerly in that town, and he may possibly be identical with the
James Rattray, writer in 'Arrol', who was a witness in Edinburgh
in 1745, for the names Rattray and Blair are both recorded in the
parish of Errol, not far east of Perth. There is later evidence that

Elizabeth's family may also have had some connection with Orkney.[1]

The responsibilities of a husband which Tytler had so rashly assumed made it urgent for him to find regular employment. He tried to practise as a surgeon; but Edinburgh had plenty of surgeons far better qualified than he. He fell back on his training under Mr Ogilvie in Forfar and set up as an apothecary. Somehow he scraped together the money to buy the necessary materials and apparatus and opened a shop for the preparation and sale of drugs in Leith, where he now settled with his wife. He counted on the custom of her acquaintances among the Glasites, but this proved disappointing, the Glasites being few and mostly poor; and meanwhile, during the short period of his enthusiasm, he neglected his business. When his interest in the Glasites faded away at about the same time as his commercial prospects, he found himself seriously in debt.

At that time a debtor who could not pay his creditors had only two choices before him, to face imprisonment or to abscond. Tytler and his wife fled from Edinburgh, beyond the jurisdiction of the Edinburgh Sheriff Court, and from Scotland, beyond that of the Court of Session. They went first to Berwick, and afterwards to Newcastle. In both places Tytler made a precarious living by 'preparing chemical medicines for the druggists'.

This is a very obscure period in Tytler's life. Its sequel hints at its miseries both economic and domestic. The five children of his marriage, none of whose births was registered in Edinburgh or Leith, must all have been born during these years of exile between 1766 and 1772, in such wretched lodgings as he could find in Berwick and Newcastle, and how he managed to keep himself and his growing family can only be imagined. He found no profitable employment, and the chances of making a rewarding living as a journeyman druggist were evidently no better in the north of England than in Scotland.

[1] The *Dictionary of National Biography*, following Paterson's statement in *Kay's Edinburgh Portraits*, says that Tytler's wife was the sister of a Writer to the Signet called James Young; but no such person existed.

In 1772, then, he returned to Edinburgh with his wife and children. Either he was able to satisfy his creditors that they had no chance of payment or they had forgotten him. He probably did not give up hope of maintaining himself by his only trade, and could earn small sums by working occasionally for established apothecaries. But from this time he began to add to his earnings by writing.

The Edinburgh to which Tytler returned was expanding both physically and intellectually. Since he left it great changes in the city's appearance had begun, which he must have surveyed with astonishment. No longer was the capital confined to its long, narrow hill. It was expanding on two sides. Spacious and elegant houses were rising in George Square and its neighbourhood southwards and in the splendidly planned New Town beyond the wide valley to the north. From the High Street, starting just below the Tron Kirk, a magnificent new bridge, carried on five lofty arches, now spanned the valley and led to the infant New Town. Beside its far end stood the new Theatre Royal, westwards from which, through what had formerly been Bearford's Parks, new houses were beginning to form the long terrace of Princes Street. Looking southwards, Tytler must have observed, day after day, scenes of varied and constant activity: mounds of earth, stacks of fresh-quarried stones, piles of scaffolding, men, horses, carts and wheelbarrows moving to and fro, some houses half-built, others completed with their smoke rising. But the whole New Town was as yet wide and low by comparison with the high-piled old city. No tower or spire yet broke the view beyond the valley towards the Forth and the hills of Fife. There was not yet a single church over there, and the Theatre Royal was so far the only public building.

For an aspiring author, the growing city offered every encouragement that activity and example could suggest. There were many printers and booksellers supplying a wide public, which spread far beyond the borders of Scotland, with books and pamphlets on every conceivable subject. The intellectual revival of Scotland was in full flower, and her authors were read and admired not only by their countrymen but in England and France.

The short time of Tytler's absence had been a period of remarkable literary fertility in Scotland, and if most of the books published during those half-dozen years are today rather reputed than read they still make an impressive list. They include Robertson's *History of the Reign of the Emperor Charles V* (actually printed in London), Boswell's *Account of Corsica*, Ferguson's *Essay on the History of Civil Society*, Beattie's *Essay on Truth* and the first part of his peom *The Minstrel*, and a widely admired novel, Henry Mackenzie's *The Man of Feeling*. The learned Lord Hailes, one of the most erudite men who ever sat on the bench of the Court of Session, was publishing a stream of small books and pamphlets containing carefully edited historical narratives and letters from old manuscripts which he unearthed in institutional or private libraries, and was pursuing the scientific study of ancient records and charters from which he was to compile his *Annals of Scotland*. From London presses appeared Sir James Steuart's *Inquiry into the Principles of Political Oeconomy* (Adam Smith's more famous work on the same subject was yet to come), an early work of the voluminous Sir John Sinclair, his *Observations on the Scottish Dialect*, and the first volume of *The History of Great Britain* by an Edinburgh minister, Dr Robert Henry. From Edinburgh presses issued various and now wholly forgotten works on theology, philosophy, history, agriculture and economics. And finally there had begun to appear, in 1771, the successive numbers of the *Encyclopaedia Britannica*, soon completed in three quarto volumes—a work with which Tytler was later to be closely associated.

Poetry rather lagged behind. At this period almost anyone could carpenter verses in the style of Pope, Thomson or Shenstone, and a great many did, in Scotland as in England, uttering commonplace sentiments in a style hackneyed in both metre and expression. No Scottish poetaster stood out from the crowded ranks of mediocrity, but some had reputations. The blind Dr Thomas Blacklock—who, like the aged and mellowed David Hume, had recently settled in

Edinburgh—was perhaps the most admired Scottish poet of this time though he now wrote little. Dr William Wilkie, whose now forgotten *Epigoniad* had once earned him (though in Scotland only) the title of 'the Scottish Homer', was on his deathbed.

But Scottish vernacular poetry still survived—loved and cherished though not taken seriously—in the old songs and ballads regularly sung at Edinburgh parties, whether in elegant chambers or in subterranean taverns and oyster-cellars; and it was beginning to revive in more literary form. Lord Hailes had in 1770 published a volume of *Ancient Scottish Poems*, including 40 poems which had never before been printed, edited from the Bannatyne Manuscript in the Advocates' Library. Two years later, at the time of Tytler's return from England, a young copyist in the office of the Clerk of the Commissary Court, Robert Fergusson, was delighting readers of *The Weekly Magazine* with his highly competent verses, some in the fashionable English modes but others lively pictures of Edinburgh street and tavern life written in the raciest vernacular and in the old Scots metres.

But much of the literature of the day was second-hand. Books being unprotected by copyright law, a public avid for knowledge was fed with innumerable extracts, digests, abridgments and translations, some in pamphlets, some in books, some in periodicals. Small printers abounded, supplying the booksellers with cheap reprints, badly produced, often from old and worn types. Edinburgh periodicals however were few. *The Weekly Magazine* had begun to appear in 1768. Firmly established since 1739 was *The Scots Magazine* which came out monthly, crammed with news, articles, anecdotes, official bulletins, vital statistics, extracts from recent books, reviews and poetry, all printed in very small type. Other magazines came and went, remaining afloat for a year or less. There were three newspapers, the *Caledonian Mercury* and the *Edinburgh Evening Courant* appearing three times a week and the *Edinburgh Advertiser* on Tuesdays and Fridays.

It was into this sub-literary world of journalism and occasional literature that Tytler found his way. At this point in his career some attempt must be made to describe the kind of man he was.

'In stature', says Meek, his first biographer, 'he was about five feet seven inches high, rather of a slender and delicate make.' His weight, on his own authority, was 140 pounds. Kay's caricature of Tytler is too small to give much idea of the countenance under the broad-brimmed hat but rather suggests a round, snub-nosed face, quite unlike the lean, lantern-jawed one of the crude woodcut reproduced by Meek which cannot possibly be an authentic likeness. Of Tytler's colouring we know nothing. His dress was careless and his whole appearance shabby, not only from poverty but from indifference.

He drifted about the streets with 'a musing, contemplative attitude', his mind probably revolving some new idea in chemistry or mechanics, some fresh foray into the world of letters, or most likely some way of raising a shilling or two for his next meal. But he could be quite a lively companion, and being a sociable creature he fell into the habit of often drinking too much. Ale, whether light or the strong, sticky 'tippenny', whisky, brandy (usually smuggled) and even claret, then imported into Scotland at a low duty under the agreeable fiction that it was a Spanish wine—all were cheap in those days.

Like many others, Tytler might have made at least a sufficient living by his pen. His talents, though limited, were by no means scanty. He had read a great deal and his head was stuffed with miscellaneous general knowledge, both literary and scientific, which seems to have been at the call of a retentive memory. But there was no particular subject on which he was really enlightened. He seems moreover to have had no literary ambition to drive him: he merely wrote to eat. He had no originality, no taste, no creative instinct, and his prose style was pedestrian. Perhaps his liveliest work was done in reviewing, for he had a certain flair for sarcastic comment which he liked to indulge. Such indulgence however earned him enemies as well as employment.

A VIEW of the NEW BRIDGE of EDINBURGH, with the adjacent buildings of the OLD and NEW TOWN, from the West

1 Edinburgh in about 1775

This was not his only failing. He had no tact and no reticence. His weaknesses were open to everyone's notice for he made no attempt to hide them. The friends he made were ill chosen. He consorted with the other inhabitants of the Edinburgh Grub Street and enjoyed what was called low company. He never received and there is no evidence that he ever sought the help of any one of the many brilliant men in Edinburgh who might have encouraged his abilities and tried to direct his wayward steps. His only patrons were the booksellers.

These businesslike tradesmen soon discovered Tytler's one useful gift, which was summarizing what other men had written. Quick and accurate, he was a born sub-editor. 'He abridged any work he took in hand with uncommon facility', says Meek, 'and separated the chaff from the wheat almost as rapidly as most men could transcribe.'

But even before he became a mere booksellers' hack, as well as frequently afterwards, Tytler attempted to become an independent writer. His first identifiable publication appeared in January 1774. If Anderson is correct in dating his return from England 'in the year 1772', there is a period of a year or more during which his pursuits are uncertain. It was, it appears, in Leith that he again found a home, and he may have made one more attempt to maintain himself and his family as a journeyman druggist. But such work of that nature as he could find would have left him time for writing as well.

By the end of 1773, at any rate, Tytler was at last embarked on a serious and indeed ambitious venture, the publication of a weekly magazine, and had found a printer for it, one William Auld. The file of this publication survives. Like all Tytler's projects it failed to stay the course, and lasted for only three months.

The Gentleman and Lady's Magazine first appeared on 28 January 1774. It is no worse than many other periodicals of its day. Much of it is quite entertaining reading and its material is various enough to have appealed to many readers. It contained paragraphs of home and foreign news, 'literary intelligence', extracts from recent books, some bad poetry, some short stories with a moral flavour, parliamentary and shipping news, and a few announcements of births, marriages and deaths.

Much of this material was obviously lifted from newspapers; but most of the essays must have been Tytler's own work, and possibly some of the verse too. It is a puzzle how and where he found access to the many books that he must have drawn upon. Another unanswerable question is what collaborators he had, for some there surely must have been. A three-page account of the production at Covent Garden of *The Man of Business*, a comedy by George Colman the elder, must have been supplied by someone with a correspondent in London. On the other hand Tytler himself probably wrote the notices of plays presented at the Edinburgh Theatre Royal. Thus in the issue of 11 February appears an uncompromisingly damning criticism of West Digges, an accomplished actor of long experience and a great favourite with Edinburgh audiences, for his performance in Colley Cibber's adaptation of Shakespeare's *Richard III*:

'Mr Digges is by no means capable for the part of Richard: he is stiff and heavy in declamation; he dresses the part ill; and seems not to conceive the sense of the author: and upon the whole, performs it rather like a lame cobler, than a deformed king.'

The dogmatic tone and crude sarcasm are very like Tytler's—as also is the inconsistency with which in the same number of the magazine he gives the highest praise to another performance by Digges, this time in Rowe's *The Fair Penitent*.

It is interesting that for the first article in the first number of his magazine, meant presumably to seize the attention of the public for which he hoped, Tytler wrote 'An Account of the Life and Writings of Dr SAMUEL JOHNSON'. It was certainly a topical subject since it was less than three months since Johnson had been in Edinburgh; and in the city's compact society, where every stranger's arrival was noted, Tytler cannot have failed to hear the great man's travels discussed. 'The world', he wrote, 'are in expectation, that

34

he will soon publish an account of the *Tour* made by him and the celebrated Mr Boswell through Scotland and the western isles in Autumn last; and surely a performance of this kind, executed by a man of his genius and observation, cannot fail in giving the highest satisfaction to every person of curiosity and taste.'

The Gentleman and Lady's Magazine had 32 pages in each issue and was published 'every Wednesday evening'. It lasted for 13 numbers and the issue of 22 April 1774 bore at the foot of its last page '*The* END *of* VOLUME FIRST'. But Volume First was also the last.

It is not likely that the magazine died because Tytler could not compass the labour of filling 32 octavo pages each week; for this was not his last attempt at a weekly magazine and, as later events showed, he was quite capable of steady and prolonged work when determined on it. Probably the magazine simply did not sell, and William Auld refused to print any more of it on credit. The public may well have found it empty of any news that it did not already know and of insufficient interest otherwise. Moreover it had a formidable rival in the *Weekly Magazine* which had in six years built up a circulation of 3000 copies and continued to flourish for another ten.

Tytler may have lost interest in his venture. He had turned once more to theology, and in this same year 1774 two books, or rather a book and a pamphlet, showed that this interest of his had not been exhausted when he left the Glasites.

The book bore the portentous but commonplace title *Essays on the Most Important Articles of Natural and Revealed Religion*, and its chief object was to combat scepticism which Tytler stigmatized as 'absurd and pernicious'. The only copy of this book that I have seen is incomplete, but according to Anderson it was abandoned when only one of two projected volumes of 'this singular work' had been printed.

The highest notoriety for scepticism at this time was enjoyed by David Hume, who was accordingly Tytler's principal target. But long before he reached the chapter 'Mr HUME Refuted' he felt obliged, in sorrow rather than in anger, to take to task Hume's most eminent Scottish opponents, Thomas Reid and James Beattie. 'I wish, indeed, I could say, that the success of these gentlemen had been equal to the goodness of their cause; but, when I view their method of arguing, and the foundation on which their reasonings are built, it appears to me, that they have left matters as they found them; that Mr Hume is still unanswered; and that his antagonists are by their own principles as much sceptics as Mr Hume himself.'

Having disposed of Beattie by a brief and scornful review of his *Essay on Truth,* Tytler declared that sceptics were unanswerable on the received philosophical principles and proceeded to give his own views on the nature of the soul and of the mind. This led him on to discuss the body too, and a digression of four pages on the circulation of the blood displayed his knowledge of anatomy if not his ability to stick to the point.

By the end of the volume he seems to have wearied of his task, or perhaps been daunted by it, and, if Anderson is right, he 'turned aside' to assault a less formidable intellect than Hume's.

During the previous year a preacher named John Barclay had appeared in Edinburgh, returning, as Tytler had done, from Newcastle. There he had obtained the ordination which the Church of Scotland had denied him on the ground of his heretical opinions. In Edinburgh he founded a religious community known as the Berean Assembly after Paul's converts in Berea, 'more noble than those in Thessalonica', who 'searched the scriptures daily'. Their ministers, according to a prejudiced contemporary, were 'mostly tradesmen, generally illiterate'. The main platform of Barclay's teaching was a denial of the possibility of natural theology, combined with the assurance of salvation to every faithful believer, who, if illuminated by the Holy Ghost, would find that everything in the Bible, in Old Testament as well as New, spoke of Christ. The Bible was the only guide to understanding, and the 'sin against the Holy Ghost' was unbelief.

Mr Barclay had set forth his views in a book entitled *The Assur-*

ance of Faith Vindicated which aroused Tytler's antagonism by its 'vehemence'. He wrote a reply to it called *The Doctrine of Assurance Considered, in a Letter to Mr Barclay* which is of interest for its light on his reasons for breaking with the Glasites as well as on his own liberal views on religion. It was not Barclay's teaching to which he objected but his dogmatism, which he compressed, not very fairly, into the blunt paraphrase 'All mankind are in a state of damnation, excepting only those few that agree with you.' He went on to castigate this attitude on general principles. 'It is the great quarrel I have with all Religious Establishments whatever *viz.* that I find among all of them an inclination to confine the Divine Favour to those of their own sect.'

There is no reason to think that Tytler had made any wide study of comparative religion. He was really thinking of his associates of 1765. 'There is no Sect, which I know of, the Papists themselves not excepted, that go such extravagant lengths in the judgement of others, as the Glasites. That Party, indeed, speaks out what other Parties do but mutter.' But even the Glasites, he went on, did not go so far as to affirm that all were damned who did not agree with them, as Barclay, complained Tytler, did: they merely maintained that they could not look on their opponents as followers of the Lord.

Tytler concluded his attack on Barclay by stating his own position. 'God is Love. . . . We are to judge of every doctrine, according to the tendency it hath to make us do good to our neighbour, or to cause us cease from loving him. . . . In this manner, I am of opinion, that we ought to judge of the doctrines of every party, and try, by no other standard than this, whether they are of God or not. I am of opinion that all the religious parties I have yet seen, are Antichrists, and think myself bound to avoid them, as I would the pestilence.'

Anderson possessed a copy of Tytler's pamphlet, probably a gift from him, which is now in the National Library of Scotland, and it was presumably from it as well as his friendship with the author that he drew his sympathetic view of Tytler's 'genuine Christianity'.

37

The *Letter* is dated at its end from 'Holy-roodhouse' and the title-page bears the imprint 'Restalrig. Printed for the Author. MDCCLXXIV. (Price Sixpence.)' But in fact both it and the *Essays* had been printed not only for but by the author, and this is the most memorable thing about them. Student, surgeon, chemist and pamphleteer, James Tytler was also a printer.

Either because he could find no printer willing to undertake his work, or from a mechanical bent of which this is the first apparent evidence, Tytler somehow constructed a printing-press of his own. There is no description of it but Meek's statement that it 'was wrought in the direction of the handle of a smith's bellows'; but it cannot have been large and must have been in some degree portable.

Both the *Essays* and the *Letter to Mr Barclay* were products of this home-made machine. Anderson remarks that Tytler's printing was 'unavoidably disfigured with many typographical deformities', and Meek goes further—'Perhaps no work was ever so much disfigured by typographical blunders.' But these criticisms are a little unjust. The standard of accuracy and the layout and setting are no worse than in many cheap publications of the period, the work of professional but inferior printers. What does betray the amateur hand, or the deficiencies of Tytler's press, is the occasional faulty alignment of type and the extreme unevenness of the inking on almost every page.

Though these various publications can have gained Tytler little profit they at any rate brought him still more to the notice of the booksellers, and he now found regular employment in supplying them with compilations, abridgments, translations and miscellaneous essays. He was able to move to somewhat better lodgings in Restalrig, a modest village two miles east of Princes Street surrounding the remains of a mediaeval church which had been cast down, as 'a monument of idolatrie', at the Reformation.

Having formed this connection with the booksellers, Tytler might well have been expected to earn a steady and sufficient living. But his bursts of industry and his considerable versatility were not directed by any sense of business. It was this lack that formed the fatal counterweight to all his abilities. He lived from hand to mouth, grasping what work was offered to him by book-sellers only too ready to take advantage of his talents, quite content that what he wrote should be anonymous or appear under other men's names, and always careless of the morrow. 'He wrote', says Anderson, 'for subsistence, not from the vanity of authorship', and subsistence meant to him the mere satisfaction of immediate needs or the payment of some more than usually troublesome creditor. He had no idea of the value of money and sold his work or his services hastily and for trifling sums. Thus, though he seemed to have found a vocation, his life was as uncertain and his affairs as em-barrassed as ever.

3

The Encyclopaedia Britannica

It is hardly surprising that after nine or ten years of marriage to her feckless husband Mrs Tytler could stand it no longer. The strain of bearing and rearing five children in a succession of grubby lodgings, beset by poverty and every kind of anxiety, must have soured her to the point where she could think only of escape. Her own account of the breaking up of her marriage, given several years later, was that she and her husband lived together till 1774 or 1775, when 'without any cause the said James Tytler totally withdrew his affection' from her and 'obliged her to leave his house'. Anderson's account is that 'his wife deserted him and their five children, the youngest only six months old, and returned to her relations'. This would be the version of the breach given by Tytler himself. But Kay's notes recorded much the same story: 'His wife, after presenting him with several children, left him to manage them as best he could, and resided with her friends, some time in Edinburgh, and afterwards in the Orkneys.'

Whoever was to blame for the rupture it was final, and clearly precipitated by Elizabeth. She set herself up in a grocer's shop in the Canongate, and there is a glimpse of her a year or two later in financial difficulties of her own. A certain Robert Ballantyne, plasterer in the Canongate, and 18 others were pursued in the Edinburgh Sheriff Court on 3 April 1776 by 'Elizabeth Rattray *alias* Tytler shopkeeper in Canongate' for payment for 'shop or grocery goods furnished by her to them'. By the end of August two of the debtors had paid up and judgment was given against the rest.

For the loss of his wife Tytler found consolation in 1779. In Paterson's account he is said to have married twice more, but this is a softening of the facts. Neither the sister of an Edinburgh flesher (i.e. butcher) named John Cairns, who shared his life for three or four years, nor her successor after 1782, Jean Aitkenhead, was married to him. By the first of these women he had one or two children before she died in childbed; and Jean Aitkenhead later made him the father of twins.

What happened to most of Tytler's progeny, legitimate or illegitimate, is unknown. But Meek, writing in 1805, knew of a daughter of Tytler's, a servant-girl in Edinburgh—'whose conduct', he says, 'I have reason to believe, is such as to be no disgrace to her most respectable connections'. Of the twins there is something to be told later.

Tytler would seem to have wished for some sort of domestic stability in his life, however trying a partner he may himself have been. His connection with Elizabeth lasted till she left him, that with the 'woman of the name of Cairns with whom he cohabited under the title or appellation of his wife for several years' until her death, and he parted from Jean, of whom Meek had heard by the name of Mrs Tytler, only briefly when obliged to flee into exile. He was a drifter and sometimes a drunkard, but he was not a rake; and it is very unlikely that he was the author of one book, certainly the work of a rake, that has been ascribed to him.

This book is of the kind described in some booksellers' catalogues as 'curious'. *Ranger's Impartial List of the Ladies of Pleasure in Edinburgh, with a Preface by a Celebrated Wit* appeared in 1775 at the price of one shilling, with the inscription 'Edinburgh. Printed for the Author.' The cynical and laboriously facetious preface is in a style that does not resemble anything known to be Tytler's. The body of the work is most unlikely to be his. It consists of a series of paragraphs describing some fifty Edinburgh whores, whose names, addresses and ages are given. Unless largely imaginary—which in view of the names and addresses is unlikely—these must be the work of someone with more leisure and much more money than Tytler ever possessed. Moreover the whole tone of this nasty little book is foreign to Tytler's nature. Sympathy for the unfortunate and a strong moral sense amounting to prudishness are discernible in many of his writings; and he was not the man to make fun of the outcasts of society as poor and as much exploited as himself.

Ranger's Impartial List is of course anonymous. The copy of it in the National Library of Scotland once belonged to Charles Kirkpatrick Sharpe and bears on its flyleaf a MS note: 'Said to be written by Balloon Tytler—CKS.' But this is not in Sharpe's handwriting. The book at any rate was certainly not printed on Tytler's home-made press.

Early in 1775 Tytler's troubles reached a climax. Possibly Elizabeth had kept some sort of order in his household and some control of its expenses which got out of hand when the deserted husband had to fend for himself. He probably still owed money to William Auld. Whatever the cause, he was now deeply in debt and threatened with prosecution. He therefore took refuge in the Abbey of Holyrood: not literally in that building which was now a roofless ruin, but in its sanctuary, the area under the jurisdiction of the Bailie of Holyrood, whose office was at this time held by Mr George Home, the Town Clerk of Leith.

The right of sanctuary in the Abbey was ancient though of uncertain origin. Formerly it had been extended to criminals, but it had long been restricted to debtors. Their right to immunity from arrest within the Sanctuary's boundaries was strictly upheld by the law, and it lasted till 1880 when imprisonment for debt was abolished. Once past the Girth Cross which used to stand near the foot of the Canongate, they were within the safe area, the boundary of which is to this day marked in the paving of the street. To leave it, if only to consult one's lawyer in the Canongate, was to risk arrest, but the debtor could remain within it as long as he chose, free from arrest, able to receive visits from friends or correspond with them, and to earn a living if he could. But he could not run up fresh debts, since retirement into the Sanctuary constituted bankruptcy in the eyes of the law, even without obtaining the Bailie's protection for which he charged a fee of two guineas.

The debtor was not too irksomely confined. The Sanctuary's area stretched for some distance east and south of the ruined Abbey and the Palace. It included Arthur's Seat and the whole of the King's Park which southwards extended to Duddingston and Newington and eastwards reached nearly as far as Jock's Lodge. What was more, on Sundays the debtor could safely leave the Sanctuary to go to church or visit his friends, for no arrest could be made on the Lord's day. But he had to be back in the Abbey by midnight on the Sunday without fail; and if he managed to slip out unobserved at any other time he could not remain absent for more than 14 days without booking himself in again for another payment of two guineas.

It was not very difficult to find a lodging 'in the Abbey' or in other words within the area of the Sanctuary, for in those days there stood within it a great many houses which have long since been removed, most of them in the middle of the last century. Some occupied the area in front of the Palace, known as the Abbey Close. On the ground south of the Palace, outside the royal garden which was later extended over and beyond it, was a group of plain, dingy houses called St Ann's Yards. The whole neighbourhood, from its consciousness of being outside the jurisdiction of the Edinburgh magistrates, had the feeling of an independent community. It was almost a little town in its own right, in which dwelt quite a number of small tradesmen, most of whom were willing to let rooms to the floating population of debtors.

They were a very motley collection, these people known in derision as 'Abbey lairds' who had paid a two guinea fee for the privilege of protection within the Sanctuary. They included not only many humble folk like Tytler but ladies and gentlemen bearing ancient and famous names, officers of the army and navy, lairds, clergymen and lawyers, English as well as Scots. The Bailie of

Holyrood's Register of Protections lists them impartially and laconically, noting for each the name, profession or trade, and address within the Sanctuary. It records the date when each debtor took sanctuary but unfortunately not the date of his departure. It shows that some of the more privileged became guests within the Palace itself where several noble families still occupied suites of rooms. Occasionally it is recorded of a debtor who was clearly not destitute that 'he has taken a house for himself'.

The Register reveals that some unlucky people took sanctuary again and again. During the last decades of the eighteenth century West Digges the actor was in the Abbey twice; so was Sir Alexander Hay, 'late captain in the 92nd regiment'; and the Master of Arbuthnott three times.

Tytler also was an 'Abbey laird' more than once. He first became one on 23 February 1775 and the Bailie's clerk, Alexander Robertson, recorded his admission thus:

'James Tytler, Chymist in Leith, last in Restalrig. Resides in Mrs Riddell's.'

On the same day the Bailie of Holyrood had also granted refuge to Lady Jean Gordon, daughter of the second Duke of Gordon, who found quarters 'in James Duncan's, vintner'. Three days earlier Andrew Cranston, wright, had likewise received as his lodger Sir William Dunbar of Hempriggs. Such were the varieties of the community of which Tytler now found himself a member and on which he cast his curious eyes. New scenes gave him new ideas and he ventured on what was perhaps his first attempt at poetry. It was a humorous ballad which he called 'The Pleasures of the Abbey'. Anderson mentions this as though it were well known but I have not been able to trace it, which is the more regrettable not only for the loss of a first-hand portrayal of life in the Abbey Sanctuary but because 'in a description of its inhabitants, the author himself is introduced in the 16th and 17th stanzas'. It would be interesting to know how Tytler regarded himself, even in the distorting mirror of a humorous ballad.

How long he stayed in the Abbey in this his first residence there is unknown. He probably continued to write. But it was not in the Abbey, as Meek and Anderson allege, that he constructed his printing-press, though he may well have taken it with him and used it there. Anderson is wrong in saying that it was from that asylum that he issued his two theological publications of 1774 which were set up on it, for the Register of Protections proves beyond doubt that he was not an 'Abbey laird' before 1775.

In a few months at most he somehow contrived to discharge or compound for his debts and was at large again, free to visit his children of whom some sympathetic friend must have assumed the care, free to hang round booksellers' doors in search of some more work of abridgment or translation, free to sit again with merry companions in the taverns of Johnny Dow or Lucky Middlemist. The search for regular work was at any rate rewarded, though that is hardly the appropriate word. Some time in 1776 Tytler embarked on the biggest, the most useful and the worst paid task of compilation that he ever undertook, which by itself entitles him to be remembered with some respect.

This was the editorship and in great part the authorship of the second edition of the *Encyclopaedia Britannica*.

Few people probably remember that the genesis of this famous work was in Edinburgh. Meek's claim that it was begun on Tytler's suggestion need not be taken seriously, for it had started to appear while he was in England and long before he was known in the literary world. It was due to the enterprise of two Edinburgh men, Colin Macfarquhar, a printer, and Andrew Bell, an engraver, came out in separate numbers at sixpence each, and was completed in three quarto volumes, the first edition running to perhaps not more than a thousand copies, though the exact number is unknown.

The plan of the *Encyclopaedia* was drawn up and all the principal articles written by William Smellie, another Edinburgh printer, the son of a stonemason. He had received some education at the parish

45

school of Duddingston and the High School of Edinburgh, but had added to it by arduous studies of his own. Before he was 30 he was a man of considerable learning, something of a chemist, with a wide knowledge of natural history and an authoritative one of botany.

Smellie was five years older than Tytler, a mild, kindly man with a witty tongue, heavy in his person, lounging in his gait and somewhat uncouth in appearance. His scholarship, acute mind and gentle nature had made him many friends, including the learned Lord Kames, and he had acquired that respect and standing in the world of letters which always eluded Tytler. He was the principal writer in a short-lived periodical, the *Edinburgh Magazine and Review*, which ran for 47 numbers between 1773 and 1776.

Smellie was a ripe character, later well known and much liked by Robert Burns; and so, in a different way, was Andrew Bell, one of the partners who engaged him for the *Encyclopaedia*. Bell was a little, knock-kneed man, so tiny in stature that he had to use a ladder to mount his horse, and made further conspicuous by an enormous, bulbous nose. This feature his odd sense of humour liked to exploit. If he met a stranger in the street who stared at it, Bell would pretend to hold it aside with one hand, asking courteously, 'Can ye win by, sir?' He carried in his pocket a false nose of monstrous size which it amused him to slip on surreptitiously over his own 'when any merry party he happened to be with had got in their cups', so as to enjoy the incredulous horror of some toper who imagined that Mr Bell's already big nose had grown much bigger since they had sat down.

Bell was by no means frivolous in matters of business, and he and Macfarquhar were well satisfied with their ambitious venture. They might indeed be so, for they had persuaded Smellie to perform the whole work of editing and abridging some articles and writing all the original ones for the total sum of £200. The first edition sold out encouragingly and they proposed to issue a second and larger one, introducing into it 'a system of general biography'. To this Smellie objected. In their original proposal the *Encyclopaedia* was to be 'a

Dictionary of the Arts and Sciences' and it was the scientific side of it that appealed to him—in particular he had written the article, which attracted much attention, on Aether. He declined to be involved in the enlarged plan, even though Macfarquhar and Bell offered him a share in the profits. The partners had therefore to look about them for a new editor.

Smellie, though not a creative writer, was one of some distinction. He had while still quite young published an edition of Terence and gained a gold medal for a treatise on botany; and he had shown his versatility and good sense in the conduct of the *Edinburgh Magazine*. He might fairly be called a man of letters, a designation which Tytler could hardly claim. Yet Tytler's capabilities might at this time have seemed, though inferior, not dissimilar to Smellie's. His fund of general knowledge was even more extensive; and he was becoming known as a very competent hand at assembling, sifting and abridging miscellaneous material. His printer Auld, an old friend of Smellie's, may have suggested Tytler as the new editor.

At any rate he was given the job, and Macfarquhar and Bell made an even better bargain than that with Smellie when Tytler agreed to undertake the second edition for the wage of sixteen shillings a week. This was the precise wage for which Smellie himself had worked from 1759 to 1765 for Murray and Cochrane, publishers of the *Scots Magazine*, as its general editor, besides 'writing accounts, and, in cases of hurry of printing, in composing, or case work'. But Smellie had accepted this modest pay when he was unknown, only 19 years old and unmarried. Tytler was now past 30, burdened with a large family and with considerable experience behind him; and the task before him was to compile not an ephemeral publication but a solid work of reference. It was not generous payment that the partners offered, especially as the *Encyclopaedia* was to be extended from the original three volumes to ten and to include a great deal of entirely new matter.

To Tytler, however, who lived from day to day, never looked ahead, and had no idea how to assess the value of his services, the bargain may have seemed quite satisfactory. Here was steady employment on work of the kind that was congenial to him, and a regular income. He settled in the village of Duddingston, some two and a half miles from Edinburgh, tucked away behind the bulk of Arthur's Seat, and devoted himself to the *Encyclopaedia Britannica*.

His children were with him in Duddingston, though not yet, if Paterson is accurate, the woman of the name of Cairns who took Elizabeth's place in his life. Sixteen shillings a week could not alone feed and clothe the family, and they lived in great poverty. Tytler could not afford a house of his own. They lodged with a washerwoman, and Tytler is said to have been obliged to use the bottom of her tub as his writing-table. What happened when his landlady needed it herself can only be guessed. The family's narrow margin between existence and starvation is illustrated by a story told to Chambers long after Tytler's death by one of his daughters, perhaps the same daughter as the respectable Edinburgh servant already mentioned. She remembered being often sent by her father from Duddingston into Edinburgh—a five-mile walk through the King's Park before she reached home again—with a small parcel of copy for the printers 'upon the proceeds of which depended the next meal of the family'. This shows that Macfarquhar and Bell's weekly wage was insufficient for Tytler and his family to live on and that he was obliged to add to it by taking on odd jobs for other employers. He himself was frugal in his habits. Meek relates that an acquaintance who called on him found him eating a cold potato 'which he continued to devour with as much composure as if it had been the most sumptuous repast upon earth'. However hampered by his poverty he was never embarrassed by it.

He laboured on the *Encyclopaedia* for six or seven years, the first of the 101 numbers of the second edition being published on 21 June 1777 and the last on 18 September 1784. Fifteen hundred copies were printed. This vast work, containing more than 9000 pages printed in double column, is conclusive evidence that Tytler, however erratic his personal affairs, was capable of steady and patient

2 Andrew Bell and William Smellie. Caricature by John Kay

application to a formidable undertaking. The mere quantity of information digested in the *Encyclopaedia* is astonishing, considering that it was almost all sought out, composed or abridged by a single man, and all of it at some stage written out in his own clear hand.

Some of the articles, such as the 36 pages on Midwifery, were taken over bodily from Smellie's work; but very many others, including the 132 pages on War, were Tytler's own. According to Anderson he wrote 'a large proportion of the more considerable scientific treatises and histories, and almost all the minor articles'. All the longer ones, following the original concept of the *Encyclopaedia*, are on pure or applied science, using the word in its widest sense. There are, to take a few examples, 32 pages given to Architecture, over 100 to Astronomy, 35 to Botany, 92 to Chemistry, 195 to Geography and 300 to Medicine. These appear to be competent and comprehensive summaries of the state of knowledge at that time of these various branches of science. Practical subjects are fully treated: Bleaching, for instance, gets ten pages and Brewing seven. Heraldry, to turn to the arts, is allotted no less than 30, besides many separate entries defining heraldic terms.

Modern history is also well served. The article on Britain and Great Britain occupies 80 pages, giving the history of the United Kingdom from 1603 down to 1763. On the other hand the treatment of ancient history is traditionally naïve and credulous, leaning confidently on the Old Testament, Herodotus and Livy as authorities. Archaeology (for which there was no entry) had not yet come to history's aid: the very word had not appeared in Dr Johnson's *Dictionary*. Among the articles which Tytler retained from the first edition is Smellie's earnest attempt to calculate the exact amount of accommodation inside Noah's Ark.

One copious entry is of particular interest for being clearly based on Tytler's own experience—the long sub-section under Fishery entitled 'Whale Fishery' which has been drawn upon in an earlier chapter. But Flying, the subject in which he was to be a practical pioneer, covers less than a page; it is concerned mostly with legendary attempts and does not mention balloons. Balloon is defined simply as 'Any spherical hollow body, of whatever matter it be composed, or for whatever purpose it be designed', and of the various purposes of balloons which are mentioned none, in the body of the work, is related to aerostatics. The treatment of the subject in the Appendix will be discussed later.

The biographies in the *Encyclopaedia*'s second edition, all added by Tytler, probably reflect with fair accuracy the opinion of his contemporaries on the comparative importance of the great figures of the past. Set beside the estimates of our own time, they are a reminder that fame is as variable as a barometer. By Tytler's assessment, Addison deserves a little more space than Shakespeare, and James Thomson about the same as Milton, and rather more than Chaucer. Martin Luther, quite appropriately, occupies nearly six pages to John Knox's one; but Locke has no more than Knox and half a page less than Hobbes, whose entry is of about the same length as Voltaire's. Nearly three pages go to Handel and rather more than one to Corelli; but Bach has no entry at all. Of the great painters, Vandyck has a whole page, more than double the allowance to Leonardo da Vinci, and Rubens gets only 25 lines, rather less than Raphael. Among famous generals Hannibal is given over a page, besides attention in the histories of Rome and Carthage. But Turenne, like Bach, has no entry, though 13 lines are given to Vauban; and their sovereign Louis XIV, with only 18 lines, is rated below his predecessor Louis IX the Crusader and saint, who gets 30.

It is probably from Tytler's lifelong interest in scientific experiment that one of the longest biographies is that of Robert Boyle, running to six pages, more than double the space given to Newton who is treated mostly as a theorist.

Anderson records that while Tytler was working on the *Encyclopaedia* he had a room assigned to him at Macfarquhar's printing-house, which was in Nicolson Street, near the University. Here Tytler combined his duties as compiler and corrector of the press. It was probably also his editorial address, for much of his material, though it was his business to abridge and arrange it, must have been furnished by experts in different fields, not all of whom, probably, were to be found in Edinburgh. The expenses of postage, which he cannot possibly have met out of his pay of sixteen shillings a week, must have been defrayed by Macfarquhar and Bell. It is extraordinary that none of Tytler's correspondence with contributors has come to light, but that there must have been such contributors seems to be proved by the portentous note on the title-page of each volume, stating that the *Encyclopaedia* has been 'compiled from the writings of the best authors, in several languages; the most approved dictionaries, as well of general science as of particular branches; the transactions, journals, and memoirs of learned societies, both at home and abroad; the MS. lectures of eminent professors on different sciences; and a variety of original materials, furnished by an extensive correspondence.'

Besides postage, Macfarquhar and Bell may be presumed to have supplied Tytler with his essential books of reference, for he can have had very few books of his own and certainly could afford to buy none. There is evidence that he did not even possess a Latin dictionary.

The first edition of the *Encyclopaedia Britannica* had had a brief and dignified title-page dated 1771 and ascribing the authorship to 'a Society of Gentlemen in Scotland'—not a very accurate description of William Smellie. It had concluded: 'Printed for A. BELL and C. MACFARQUHAR; And sold by COLIN MACFARQUHAR, at his Printing-office, Nicolson-street.' The title-page of the second edition, dated 1778, mentioned no author or authors. It credited the publication to a consortium of printers, to whom in all probability Macfarquhar had been obliged to farm out some of the work which had proved to be beyond his resources—J. Balfour & Co., W. Gordon, J. Bell, J. Dickson, C. Elliot, W. Creech, J. McCliesh, A. Bell, J. Hutton, and C. Macfarquhar.

Above this parade of printers' names the title-page was verbose and pompous. Instead of being merely 'compiled upon a New Plan', the *Encyclopaedia* was now, it announced, 'on a PLAN entirely NEW' and stated to contain 'Various detached parts of knowledge . . . Ecclesiastical, Civil, Military, Commercial, &c. Together with a Description of all the Countries . . . throughout the World; a General History . . . of the different Empires, Kingdoms, and States; and an Account of the Lives of the most Eminent Persons in every Nation.' This proclamation of the contents was followed by the summary of their sources already quoted. The whole page was an advertisement of the work, and was printed verbatim by the *Scots Magazine* by way of a review in its October number, the month after the last section of the *Encyclopaedia* had appeared. All it added at the top of the column which this material took up was the short announcement—

'This voluminous work, which contains upwards of 9000 pages, is now finished. Number 1 was published on June 21, 1777, and Number 181, which is the last, on Sept. 18, 1784; so that it has been more than seven years in the press.'

The *Scots Magazine* did not take note of the *Encyclopaedia*'s inclusion of little Mr Bell's engravings, clear, delicate and beautiful, of which there were more than 300. There was no commendation of the work, and no mention of the industrious editor.

Tytler's achievement none the less became known in Edinburgh and was not forgotten, at least for a few years. Even so demanding a task as editing a ten-volume encyclopaedia had not absorbed the whole of his energies. At least two other major enterprises he undertook as side-lines during this period, driven, no doubt, by the urgency of his family's needs. In 1780 he started another magazine, *The Weekly Mirror*, each issue of which contained 16 octavo pages of essays, stories and historical digests. The first number appeared on Friday, 22 September 1780, the last on 23 March 1781. The magazine was printed by J. Mennons & Co., Brodie's Close, Lawnmarket. There were some gaps in the issue of 2 February. 'The Publishers', it announced, 'presents [*sic*] compliments to the

Readers of the Weekly Mirror, and hopes they'll excuse the want of the LITERARY MEMOIR this week, as the AUTHOR's indisposition prevented him from finishing it, as well as from concluding the story of THE SEDUCER PUNISHED.' This lurid though moral tale was hastily rounded off in the next number, but that of 16 February contained an apology for its late appearance as due to the same cause, though it added that 'the Author of the Mirror is now considerably better'. He was 'fully recovered', it was announced in the issue of 23 March, but evidently incapable of carrying on the magazine, which was abruptly wound up. Its publication in a single volume included an index page, on the back of which appeared a note stating that 'the *indisposition* of the Author' and the impossibility of finding a substitute for him had caused its cessation. The italicised word possibly indicated another explanation to those who knew Tytler.

The *Weekly Mirror* of 2 February mentioned that there had been some 'censures' of the magazine by 'our friend the Tinklarian'. The allusion is to a notorious Edinburgh character of half a century earlier, one William Mitchel, a 'tinkler' or tinker in the West Bow who, in a torrent of discursive and abusive pamphlets over many years, had styled himself the Tinklarian Doctor and even the Professor of Tinklarianism. Someone presumably had been writing against Tytler in a style which he chose to ridicule by this epithet.

Tytler is said to have written occasionally for another short-lived periodical, the *Edinburgh Evening Post*, which started in May 1780 and was still in existence in October 1781. But some months after the collapse of the *Weekly Mirror* he embarked on another project of his own, possibly suggested to him by his work in compressing history for articles in the *Encyclopaedia Britannica*. He set himself to abridge the *Universal History*, a vast work published by three London booksellers of which the second edition, issued in 1747–8, ran to 20 octavo volumes. It covered ancient and early mediaeval history down to the fall of Constantinople in 1453, and Tytler had found it useful as a quarry for *Encyclopaedia* material.

This time he did not sell his anonymous labours. He proposed not only to execute the work himself but to reap the whole credit and the whole profits, and he turned again to his home-made printing-press. His *General History of All Nations, Ancient and Modern* never got beyond one volume of 396 pages, but that bore on its title-page the words 'By J. Tytler' and its imprint read 'printed by the Author and sold by D. Oliphant, bookseller, West Bow'.

The *General History*'s actual contents are not impressive. The Introduction gives a very vague sketch of world geography, based, one would almost think, either on memory or on a single small-scale map. Thus of countries neighbouring to the British Isles we learn, 'Almost directly north is the island of Iceland, distant more than 600 miles; north-east, at the distance of 1500 miles, are the frozen islands of Spitzbergen, where our ships go to the whale-fishery; and farther to the south are the northern parts of Russia and Lapland.'

A few items of curious information are included, such as that Gibraltar 'stands on a high rock; and what is very extraordinary, great part of this rock is found to be composed of human bones, concerning which philosophers have speculated much but to no great purpose'. This observation does not come from the *Universal History* and is one of Tytler's personal touches, of which another example is the following innocent, not to say complacent reflection:

'The invention of fire-arms rendered it impossible to make such rapid conquests as formerly, because now the art of war is reduced to certain rules, which are very generally known, and is besides carried on with such weapons as render defence in a great measure vain. . . . There is, therefore, very little danger of such revolutions and disturbances as have taken place in ancient times; and the nations now existing seem to be established on a much more permanent basis than even those empires which have made the greatest figure in history.'

The *History*'s one completed volume does not get beyond the treatment of the Babylonians, the Medes and Persians, and the Greek states down to the death of Alexander the Great. In ancient Attica, we are told, 'the power of the archons was restricted in the year [in] which Hezekiah king of Judah was born, about 752 B.C., after which the authority continually diminished, till at last it dwindled into a downright democracy'—a startling conclusion until we recollect that in Tytler's day democracy was becoming a pejorative term equivalent to mob-rule. But even for democracy in its modern sense he seems to have had no great admiration at this time, to judge by his patronizing account of the Athenians in the most glorious period of their history:

'Though they were sufficiently fond of war, yet they encouraged painting, sculpture, oratory, and many kinds of polite learning. They were a thoughtless and giddy people, always running from one enterprise to another, perpetually aspiring to be great without being able to lay down any solid permanent plan by which they could accomplish their wishes.—As to true virtue they appear to have been as great strangers to it as the Lacedemonians or any other state whatever.'

Yet this production of Tytler's, however superficial and naïve, really deserves notice for the extraordinary manner of its composition. 'It is well known to many', writes Meek, 'that without any manuscript, with the universal history lying open before him, and setting the types with his own hand, he abridged as he went on, with as much ease as if he had not been making the smallest alteration on a single sentence.' Anderson, who does not include the *General History* among such works of Tytler's as he mentions, records the same fact about Tytler's *Essays* of 1774—'composed by himself, at the printing case, from his own conceptions, without a manuscript before him, and wrought off at a press of his own construction, by his own hands'. This may also have been true: Tytler may have asserted it to Anderson himself. But Meek's account, attaching this feat to the *General History* alone, has the ring of conviction, as though gathered from someone who had actually seen the shabby little author standing 'with the universal history open before him' at his rough but practical printing-press, presumably set up in the washerwoman's house in Duddingston, and working away as composer and compositor at once.

Like the *Essays* and the *Letter to Mr Barclay*, the *General History* is not quite fairly censured as 'disfigured with many typographical deformities'. There are certainly a few misprints—not nearly so many as commonly appear in a modern newspaper's first edition—but the book is quite tidily and accurately printed, the pages competently laid out, and the uneven inking of the type, though noticeable, much less pronounced than in the earlier books. However, 'THE END OF THE FIRST VOLUME' was also the end of this project. Tytler's reason for abandoning it, Meek guessed, was 'his want of perseverance, or perhaps his domestic necessities'. More probably even Tytler found that he could not spare enough time from satisfying Macfarquhar's demands for copy for the *Encyclopaedia Britannica*, especially to carry on a work for which he was receiving no payment while it continued and which seemed likely to find few buyers when it was completed.

None the less his regular toil for Macfarquhar and Bell—the reading, the digesting, the writing to contributors and sifting of their material, the drafting (if he did make drafts) and the copying—did not exhaust Tytler's enterprise. In 1781 he made another venture in poetry. 'He sometimes', as Meek puts it, 'paid court to the Muses'; but it must be admitted that the goddesses were either deaf or inattentive whenever Tytler sought their help.

He embarked on a translation into English heroic couplets of Virgil's *Eclogues*. Like so many others of his projects this one was never finished; he completed only the first four of the ten. These he printed himself, really quite elegantly, and got Mr Elliot, a bookseller in Parliament Square, one of the group concerned in the *Encyclopaedia Britannica*, to publish the thin quarto at two shillings a copy. It was dedicated to William Charles Little of Liberton, the head of an old Edinburgh family settled for the last 250 years on a small estate not far outside the city, 'in token of gratitude for favours unmerited and unsolicited'. This is the sole evidence that someone of position had shown Tytler some encouragement, but there is none of what it was. Little had a house in Brodie's Close, off the Lawnmarket, where Tytler's *Weekly Mirror* had been printed.

Virgil as rendered by Tytler resembles Bottom after undergoing the attentions of Puck, 'translated indeed'. In a preface he explains his method: 'Of all the authors of antiquity, none hath baffled the efforts of translators more than our celebrated Mantuan Poet. The author of the present translation hath been induced to make the attempt, not from an opinion of his own skill in the Latin language, but from observing the reason of such remarkable failures in others.' This, it appears, was the vain attempt to stick too closely to the original. 'The author of the present translation hath chosen to follow the sentiment rather than the language of Virgil. . . . Hence the reader will find many deviations from the mere words of the original, but none from the sentiment.'

The final claim was however thrown overboard as soon as the translator got to the second eclogue, which he found embarrassing. 'The poet', he observed in the Argument prefixed to his version, 'expresses an unnatural passion for a boy, according to the infamous custom of the Romans in his time. The translator, however, to accommodate the poem to the chaste ears of Christian readers, hath substituted the name of a girl. By this alteration the beauty of the original can lose nothing, and every one can enter into the spirit of such a poem, though few, it is hoped, could do so in the other.' With this tactful precaution Tytler went ahead, rendering *Formosum pastor Corydon ardebat Alexin* as

> *Young Corydon for fair Alicia burn'd*

and proceeding accordingly.

Since the translation generally gives a whole English couplet to each Latin hexameter, the 'sentiment' of Virgil benefits a good deal from Tytler's need to fill up his lines. He could not, for example, be so economical as the Mantuan Poet with the conclusion of eclogue

III—*Claudite jam rivos, pueri; sat prata biberunt*—which became

> *Now shut the sluices, now your contest end,*
> *Lest too much wet the tender grass offend.*

All in all, his talent for tumbling into bathos had ample scope.

What Mr Little thought of the *Eclogues* can only be imagined, though it is to be hoped that he brought himself to acknowledge a complimentary copy politely. In another quarter they had no such reception. Tytler confidently sent a copy to a critic whose identity Meek conceals under initials and who returned it with contemptuous rudeness. Tytler was stung. He retorted at once with 'a ludicrous poem' which has not survived. Meek says it was 'as coarse as the reply which gave it birth, and full of the most pointed satire'.

He had another shot at Virgil, none the less, the following year in another thin quarto: 'The Hermit: a Sacred Eclogue, in imitation of the Sixth Pastoral of Virgil intitled Silenus. To which is added a Translation of that Pastoral into English Verse. By J. Tytler. Printed by the Author, and sold by D. Oliphant, Bookseller, head of the West Bow. 1782.'

The *Sacred Eclogue* is a poem about a hermit living in a remote part of India and discovered unexpectedly there by a party of travellers. To them he sings of the creation of the world, the flood, and several articles of sacred history, at very much greater length than Silenus recounts his Greek legends in the original, but much more edifyingly. A single example from this piece is enough to illustrate both its quality and Tytler's passion for science—even at the most inappropriate moments. The Hermit's vision of the Day of Judgement reaches its climax in these striking lines:

> *For thunder's voice is lost in pow'r divine,*
> *And pointless lightnings now forget to shine.*
> *Convolv'd like scrolls depart the fleeting skies,*
> *And ev'n the strong Electric Ether dies.*

In poetry as in other ventures, Tytler strove to rise, always optimistic, always confident that whatever other men had done he could do, but always fated to sink. The pattern was to be repeated in the one memorable project of his life.

4

The Grand Edinburgh Fire Balloon—I

It must have been in the winter of 1783 that Tytler became seriously interested in balloons. They had in the last few months become a subject widely discussed, not only by scientists but by the general public. The idea of the aerial balloon, filled with either hot air or hydrogen ('inflammable air'), had been, so to speak, floating about for several years, and unmanned balloons, quite small in size, had been released in numerous experiments. In 1783 speculation turned to the possibility of large balloons that might actually lift a man into the air and enable him to navigate even that unfamiliar element.

The French were the pioneers of the new science of aerostation, and the generally recognized inventors of the manned balloon are the two brothers Montgolfier, Joseph and Etienne, papermakers of Annonay near Lyons. After successful trials with models they constructed a large balloon of cloth and launched it, filled with hot air, at Versailles on 19 September 1783, carrying the first balloonists to leave the surface of the earth. These however were not human, being a cock, a duck and a sheep, who rose to a height of some 1500 feet and came safely down two miles away.

A month later, on 25 October, the world's first aeronaut rose from Paris in another Montgolfier balloon—J. F. Pilâtre de Rozier. This balloon was a captive one and was allowed to rise only 80 feet, but the experiment was sufficiently reassuring. On 21 November Pilâtre de Rozier made a free flight to a height of about 300 feet and to a distance of five and a half miles, accompanied by a passenger, the Marquis d'Arlandes. This historic journey was made with a balloon filled with hot air by means of a brazier carried below the neck which actually set fire to the envelope during the flight, but the aeronauts suppressed the danger with a wet sponge.

Meanwhile the brothers Robert were experimenting with a hydrogen balloon with an envelope fabric of silk and rubber, and moreover devising the essential features of valve, net, suspended car and ballast. Their balloon's first flight, made from the Tuileries by one of the brothers and a young physicist named Charles, lasted for two hours and extended to no less than 9,000 feet of height and 27 miles of distance.

It was now clear that balloons were practical vehicles of flight. The craze for 'Montgolfières' and 'Charlières', as the hot air and hydrogen types were respectively termed, spread quickly, and successful ascents were made early in 1784 in other parts of France and in Italy. News of them was widely reported and it is clear that Tytler read it avidly. During the summer of 1784 he was at work on the last volume of the *Encyclopaedia Britannica* containing the Appendix which was issued to the public in September. He took the opportunity to enlarge the earlier entry on Air and included in it a new section on Air Balloons extending to over eight pages. Since this entry while describing recent ballooning experiments quoted one report of March 1784, it was thoroughly up to date. 'By this invention', Tytler wrote, 'the schemes of transporting people through the atmosphere, formerly thought chimerical, are realized; and it is impossible to say how far the art of aerial navigation may be improved, or with what advantages it may be attended.' He expressed his opinion that 'inflammable air' was 'most eligible' for merely experimental balloons, and hot air—'air passing through fire'—for balloons 'of the higher kind, where some person ascends with them'.

Long before he wrote these lines Tytler had resolved to make an ascent in a hot air balloon himself. Incapable of reticence as he was, he must have talked openly of his desire and even his intention during the spring of 1784, for it is to that year that a paper must belong making satirical allusion to his scheme. This survives in a scrapbook kept by Dugald Stewart, Professor of Moral Philosophy in the University of Edinburgh. It is neither dated nor signed, and I have not identified its bold handwriting. It was probably an after-dinner jest handed about some gathering of University wits, a parody of a typical newspaper advertisement:

'We have authority to assure the Public that it is neither Mr Tytler of Woodhouselee nor Mr Frazer Tytler Advocate and Professor of Civil History in the University of Edinburgh that means to go up with the Air Balloon on the 7th of May, but Mr James Tytler an ingenious Chemist and distant relation of the others, whose friends it is hoped will accept of this Intimation of their having no intentions of going up with air balloons at present, what evermalicious or interested persons may chuse to give out, or credulous people may believe.'

In the British Isles ballooning was at this time still confined to sending up unmanned models, mere toys, like the one exhibited by a Swiss scientist to George III at Windsor Castle in November 1783, inflated by 'un fort joli appareil'. This, which the King played with for some time at the end of a string and watched after its final release for ten minutes until it disappeared in the sky, was only 30 inches in diameter. Although larger balloons were being projected in Great Britain in early 1784 and there was much talk about them, both serious and satirical, no one had yet managed to make or mount in one. As late as 2 September 1784 a journalist lamented: 'It is now almost 12 months since Montgolfier first ascended, yet England, with all its learning, ingenuity and encouragement of the arts, has never been able to produce one John Bull who wishes to take an airing this way.'

For England that was still true, although James Sadler, the first English aeronaut, was to make a successful ascent at Oxford on 4 October. But in Scotland he was anticipated by more than five weeks.

The planning of Tytler's attempt must have been begun in the spring of 1784, to judge by the jocular allusion to it already quoted. From later reports it is clear that he raised a subscription towards it, though by what efforts or with how much success is as unknown as are the names of his subscribers. It was at any rate barely enough for his needs. His project, as we have seen, was being talked of in May and in the middle of June he made his first bid for public attention to it, with the motive of stimulating further subscriptions. On 19 June, a Saturday, the first advertisement of Tytler's balloon appeared in the *Edinburgh Evening Courant*, prominently placed at the top of a column on the front page:

On Monday next, the 21st current, will be exhibited
AT COMELY GARDEN
By JAMES TYTLER, CHEMIST,
A FIRE BALLOON, of 13 Feet in Circumference,
AS A MODEL OF
THE GRAND EDINBURGH FIRE BALLOON,
with which he intends to attempt the Navigation of
the Atmosphere.
As this Exhibition is intended to give the Public a demonstration of the principles upon which the Great Balloon will ascend, it is not necessary to confine it to any particular hour.—The balloon will therefore be repeatedly exhibited from Eleven o'clock forenoon till Three afternoon, and from Four till Seven in the evening.
Admission Sixpence. Subscribers.—Gratis.
∴ As this balloon will be confined by a string,
its ascent cannot be seen by any person
except those admitted into the Garden.

The last paragraph, designed to encourage the flow of sixpences from the curious, is a reminder that Comely Garden was surrounded by a wall, lined inside by trees. The place lay north-east of Holyrood near the old London road, just south of the line of the present railway. It was a pleasure garden containing a pavilion, which had a not very successful career of about 30 years, having been first opened in January 1758 with a 'grand ball' and a display of fireworks.

Comely Garden had had its brief period of fashion. It was there in 1767 that the beautiful though hoydenish Jane Maxwell had been dancing when she captivated the rich and handsome Duke of Gordon whom she soon afterwards married. But fashion had long deserted it. Writers on Edinburgh dismissed it with a sniff of contempt as a wretched imitation of Vauxhall, and the occasional visitor found it dull and half empty with only four or five musicians in place of an orchestra. Various managers had failed to lure the fashionable public back again. The last of these, Alexander Williamson, took it over in May 1784, announcing that entertainments would be given in the ballroom every Tuesday and Saturday. He was no doubt delighted to welcome Tytler's balloon as affording Comely Garden some additional publicity. From Tytler's point of view the place was well chosen. Edinburgh, standing on high ground near the sea, was a windy city, and shelter for the balloon was essential. Comely Garden, lying to the south of Abbey Hill, was sufficiently protected by it and Calton Hill from the north-west winds, and was also a well-known place of public resort, even if not very popular, quite close to the city.

There is no report of how many Edinburgh citizens paid their sixpences to watch the 13 foot balloon make its modest ascents, 'confined by a string', to a height perhaps just great enough to tantalize the non-paying who were outside the Garden. But Tytler was encouraged to continue his scheme. It was at any rate in the news. A week after his exhibition the *Edinburgh Evening Courant*'s issue of 28 June made a passing allusion to it when reporting the successful flight at Rouen of another French balloonist, Blanchard—'M. Blanchard has got the start of our intended aerial navigator Mr Tytler'. By the middle of July Tytler had constructed his full-sized balloon and made some experimental inflations of it, though it was not really finished. Where this work was carried on is uncertain. Possibly it was in some corner of Comely Garden.

Fowls of a Feather Flock together.

3 'Fowls of a Feather Flock Together'. Caricature by John Kay
Lunardi in the centre faces Tytler, whose balloon is shown on
the left

No verbal description has survived of 'the Grand Edinburgh Fire Balloon', and we can infer its form and construction from little evidence but that of a small engraving which must have been drawn either by Tytler himself or someone working under his eye (see frontispiece). The crude representation of Tytler's balloon in Kay's caricature was obviously drawn from hearsay only. It was not spherical but approximately barrel-shaped; and the envelope, made of cloth, probably linen, was not enclosed by a net but by a kind of open framework of cables drawn in below to suspend a boat-shaped car which probably never progressed beyond the stage of design. The thing looked like what it was sometimes called, a machine. Its aspect was severely practical, and in this respect it differed from all the other early balloons which were extremely decorative. Whether their projectors were moved by the spirit of science or merely of adventure, their chance of public interest and influential patronage hung on the balloon's value as entertainment. So the great globes that soared into the air were gorgeously decked with patterns in bright colours, figures of gods and goddesses, the signs of the zodiac, stars, mottoes and coats of arms. The 'chariot' that swung below a 'Charlière' was a splendid vehicle shaped like a romantic shallop, and the 'gallery' beneath the neck of a 'Montgolfière' was hardly less picturesque, while the aeronaut ascending in either type was careful to include in his equipment a suitable flag to wave to the spectators of his triumph. But Tytler had no money to spend on such fancies.

Indeed he was so short of funds that the summer dragged on without his being able to complete the full-sized balloon that he had designed. The subscription list had been filled with names but few of those who had signed it had paid their contributions, the notion being current that these need not be produced till after a successful flight. Tytler's resources were enough to make the balloon itself but not to construct the framework by which he designed to have it supported during inflation before flight. A further obstacle which he could not have foreseen now appeared—actual opposition to the flight itself. A rumour came to his ears that it would be forbidden by authority for fear of causing a mob.

Caution therefore as well as lack of funds enforced some postponement of the balloon's launch. Tytler resolved to attempt it during the race week in August when crowds would at any rate be expected so that he could not be accused of attracting them. In the interval he tried to keep interest in his project alive and attract more subscribers by another preliminary exhibition. He inserted the following advertisement in the *Edinburgh Evening Courant* where it appeared prominently on 17 July 1784:

EDINBURGH FIRE BALLOON

The Gentlemen who have subscribed, or who intend to subscribe, for the Edinburgh Fire Balloon, are requested to attend at the Register Office, New Town, on Monday forenoon, in order to see it filled, and to give their opinion as to what is further necessary to be done before its removal from the place, where it now is.

The 'Register Office' was the projected but unfinished General Register House, the proposed repository for the public records of Scotland which had long before overflowed their quarters in the Laigh Parliament House. Many were at this time scattered in various makeshift stores in different parts of Edinburgh. Their dispersal and neglected condition had been a national scandal since the Union and indeed since the Restoration; but it had moved only a few to protest and remedial action had taken long to arrive and was still moving very slowly. A Royal warrant for the erection of the General Register House had been obtained by James, 14th Earl of Morton, Lord Clerk Register, in 1765, but the foundation stone had not been laid till 1774 by his successor in office Lord Frederick Campbell, the Duke of Argyll's brother, and the funds appropriated for the building had been inadequate. For some years work on it had been at a standstill and the magnificent structure designed by Robert Adam stood half-finished and roofless, derisively known as 'the largest pigeon-house in Europe'.

The Register House was nearly opposite the Theatre Royal, exactly fronting the northern end of the new North Bridge. Its site had been carefully chosen to make it a focal point of the New Town and encourage the taking up of feus[1] in that quarter of it. But no buildings were as yet erected or even planned on its north-east side where St James's Square was later built but where feus were not even advertised before December of this year. The Register House, a few yards beyond the eastern end of Princes Street, was virtually outside the New Town, a desolate and untidy place. Mounds of earth excavated from the foundations still lay around it. Clouds of dust blew in dry weather along the unfinished Princes Street to the west, half of which was still unpaved. The unglazed windows of the Register House stared blank and mournful from its three completed sides and in the middle the great dome stood open to the sky.

In the minutes of the Trustees for the building of the Register House there is a regrettable gap at this period; they apparently held no meetings until the work was resumed, with a fresh advance from Government funds, in 1785. It is therefore impossible to say how Tytler gained permission, or from whom, to use the incomplete building for the assembly and trial inflation of his balloon. Yet this, it appears from the advertisement just quoted, is what he seems to have done.

It was a very practical plan. Shelter was imperative for the experimental filling of the balloon with hot air, and not easy to find outdoors for so large an object. According to Paterson, the only writer to note the dimensions of Tytler's balloon, it was 40 feet high and 30 feet wide. Thus it could easily be got into the Register House dome of which the internal diameter was 50 feet. No place in Edinburgh could have suited Tytler's purpose better.

Among the spectators who came to the Register House on 19 July were reporters from the *Edinburgh Advertiser* and the *Courant*, whose accounts, though sympathetic, show that the experimental

[1] Perpetual leaseholds.

inflation did not go very well. Previous trials had clearly filled the envelope with smoke as well as hot air, and a quantity of soot had collected on its inner surface. Tytler started his furnace a little before noon and the envelope began to 'swell very considerably'; but the rush of hot air carried up into it some sparks which before the inflation was complete had burnt several small holes in it. The fire was hastily extinguished and Tytler put a brave face on the mishap. He thought the accident a very material advantage, he said, for he had learnt some important facts from it; and the damage could easily be repaired. He did not withdraw an impressive advertisement which he had drawn up for the *Edinburgh Advertiser* and which appeared the following day on the page facing the paper's account of the Register House experiment.

It had been deliberately timed. Four days earlier the Edinburgh papers had published the usual intimation of the races to be run 'over the sands of Leith' and this year to take place from Monday the 2nd to Saturday the 7th August. Leith Races were one of the great social events of the Edinburgh year, drawing to the city crowds of people of all classes. There would be balls and assemblies for the gentry; hawkers, buskers and cheapjacks to entertain the commonalty; good business for brewers and vintners and the promise of trouble for the City Guard, as poor young Robert Fergusson had described a decade earlier in one of his liveliest Scots poems. There could be no better time for Tytler to make his great bid for public attention than the opening day of the races after the running of the three four-mile heats for the City of Edinburgh's Plate; and there would be five days thereafter in which to repair any disappointment or consolidate success. His advertisement was filled with promise and confidence, despite his continued anxiety about the financing of his venture.

EDINBURGH FIRE BALLOON

To be exhibited as formerly advertised, on Monday 2d of August next, and during the greater part of the Race Week. On Monday it will be exhibited immediately after the Race; and on each of the succeeding days, at the hour determined by the Company of the preceding day, that they may accommodate themselves with the race, and a further view of the Balloon, if they think proper. On the first days of the week it will be suffered to ascend only with ropes, that such company as come into town on account of the race, may have an opportunity of observing its principles and powers. On Friday at eleven o'clock forenoon, if the wind blows not directly towards the sea, it will be set at liberty, and J. Tytler, as formerly advertised, will accompany it. If the wind should prove unfavourable on Friday, this exhibition will be attempted on Saturday, and if still unfavourable, on the first day when it blows from the east, north or south, so that the Balloon may either cross the Frith of Forth, or fly over the inland parts of the country. A flag on the Observatory on the Calton-hill, will inform the public of the day on which the Balloon is to be set at liberty.

As a few of the Subscribers have not paid in their Subscription money, it is hoped they will not take it amiss, if they are waited on with Receipts; and as experiment has determined that some alterations in the Stove, Basket, &c, are necessary to prevent accidents, the farther assistance of the public is solicited, the whole sum as yet subscribed being insufficient to defray the expence.

Subscriptions for J. Tytler taken by Mr Elliot, Parliament Square, and the Royal Exchange Coffee-house. The particular place of exhibition will be previously advertised.

The race week approached and Edinburgh filled up for it with visitors from all around. Some of them read, with nostalgic recollection of memorable nights at the Theatre Royal and elsewhere, of West Digges's death in Dublin 'of a violent fever'. Numerous attractions were offered to the pleasure-seekers. In the large room below Balfour's Coffee-house in Parliament Square 'The Amazing Little Woman' was on view, 26 years old and weighing less than 18 pounds. By contrast Mr Robertson, ladies' hairdresser at No. 2 Princes Street, was exhibiting two giant twins, 23 years old and 'very near EIGHT FEET HIGH'. But what were giants and dwarfs compared to the real novelty of the Edinburgh Fire Balloon? Tytler repeated his advertisement in the *Courant* of Saturday 31 July, two days before the race week opened.

The place of the balloon's ascent was now announced as once again Comely Garden. Otherwise the advertisement was in much the same terms as before, repeating that, after the captive ascents, the balloon would, weather permitting, be set at liberty on the Friday—'and J. TYTLER will accompany it'. There were however two additional paragraphs. Subscribers of half a guinea and upwards would be admitted to Comely Garden at all times. Otherwise admission would be by ticket, valid on the day when presented and also 'on the day that J. Tytler accompanies the Balloon'. One of these tickets has survived (see frontispiece). It shows that each was numbered, and signed by Tytler himself. Each was also a further small advertisement, for it carried an engraving depicting the balloon, made the more impressive by its exaggerated size in comparison with the tiny human figure in the car below.

Further, J. Tytler offered his respectful compliments to the commanding officer of the regiment in the Castle 'for his polite behaviour in offering a guard of the military, to prevent any disturbance to the Ladies and Gentlemen that may attend the different exhibitions'.

And then, for another week, not a word about the Edinburgh Fire Balloon appeared in the newspapers.

In fact, Tytler's preparations, hampered by lack of funds, were incomplete and inadequate. To hold up the balloon while it was being inflated he had designed a lever 64 feet long fixed to the top of a mast 50 feet in height so that the balloon would be held just clear of the ground and the fire below it. The mast, perhaps because he had not been able to afford one stout enough, was too thin, and on the Sunday, the day before the race week began, it broke. The balloon therefore could make no ascent on the Monday. It was too late to advertise a postponement. After a horse called Come-if-ye-can had won the City of Edinburgh's Plate, a crowd assembled at Comely Garden only to be disappointed.

The next trouble was the weather. Though the damaged mast

was repaired or replaced, nothing could be done for the next three days. Comely Garden was sheltered from the north and north-west but not from the west, and it was from that quarter, not unusually, that a strong wind blew for most of the race week. Tytler had the balloon and its apparatus removed to a somewhat better sheltered place in another part of the Garden, and on the Friday evening, the day on which he had undertaken to make a free flight and when perhaps a larger number of spectators than usual had assembled, he had the balloon inflated. But the wind was still too strong. The bulging mass swayed violently to and fro, tugging at the ropes by which Tytler's men restrained it and obviously quite unstable. The 'gallery' was damaged and some of the cords suspending it broken. Once more the attempt at flight was abandoned.

The following evening the *Courant* printed a brief and unkind paragraph: 'The Edinburgh Fire Balloon has been struggling hard to make its public appearance during the race week. Masts and yards and scaffolds and furnaces have lent their aid, but to little purpose. Its gravity and affection for the earth cannot be overcome.'

But public expectation had been excited by these failures, and while this paragraph was in the press a crowd was watching the desperate attempt that Tytler made to fulfil his promise to make a balloon ascent during the week of Leith Races. On that Saturday evening between five and six o'clock the wind was at last dying down and once more he had his balloon hoisted up its mast and inflated. He was actually about to step into the hastily repaired 'gallery' when the wind suddenly freshened. In the words of the *Caledonian Mercury* a week later: 'A gust of whirlwind, as if sent by divine command to blast the hopes of this devoted projector, attacked the Balloon, drove it hither and thither, and by compressing it on all sides, soon reduced it to a state of flaccidity; some rents were made, which prevented any further attempt that night.'

There was a howl of disappointment as the balloon collapsed. Mobs do not reason, and a mob cheated of a promised amusement can be blindly savage. A mob indeed was all this gathering probably was, on a Saturday evening with the races over, the scum of the race crowd reinforced by the scallywags of Edinburgh, and many of them doubtless drunk. Tytler took himself out of the way as quickly as possible before the crowd closed in. After a brief search they forgot him and turned on the balloon. They did not fortunately destroy the great crumpled bag but they broke up the wicker basket which was to have carried Tytler in his 'gallery' and burned it on the fire which was still glowing.

The *Edinburgh Advertiser*, which on the Friday had devoted a whole column to reporting another successful balloon ascent in France, this time by the brothers Robert and the Duc de Chartres at St Cloud, rubbed in Tytler's failure on the Tuesday following by reprinting the brief and contemptuous paragraph about it from the *Courant*. But the *Caledonian Mercury*, on Saturday the 14th, gave considerable space to a not unsympathetic account of the scheme and its setback, emphasizing that Tytler had by no means abandoned it but was determined to accomplish his purpose, and drawing attention to 'the very slender support which the scheme had received from the public'.

Tytler examined his balloon and set to work to repair it. The envelope had suffered a good deal, first from the small burns received in the Register House and recently from slight tearing. These rents could be mended but the envelope could no longer be trusted as airtight. It had been given a paper covering and this was now in so tattered a state that Tytler decided to remove it altogether and give the envelope a coat of varnish instead. This was done and 'one of the small baskets in which earthen ware is carried'—to quote Tytler's own description of it—was procured to take the place of the destroyed car. But the rest of the 'gallery' was gone and the balloon was not now equipped to carry the stove, which weighed nearly 300 pounds.

The whole contrivance really needed re-building. But Tytler was desperately short of money and moreover desperately short of time. He could not hope to keep his small crew of assistants together much longer, and if he were to maintain the fast diminishing public interest in his venture he must make a flight very soon. It would have to be reduced to its essentials, the demonstration that a light vessel filled with hot air could ascend from the earth and, if large enough with sufficient power, lift a man with it. There would be no gallery, no stove, no ballast: only the balloon, the hot air, the small basket and J. Tytler.

It was, as he wrote afterwards, 'the resolution of a madman, and which nothing but my desperate situation could excuse'. But for the moment it was the only alternative to complete abandonment of the Edinburgh Fire Balloon. Tytler laboured to repair the envelope and to apply its coat of varnish which he hoped, though 'a proper composition could not be afforded', would prove serviceable. In a fortnight he was ready.

But soon after the middle of August another topic began to fill space in the Edinburgh press, and Tytler lost the advantages of occasional paragraphs to keep the public interested in his plans. A new Member of Parliament for the city was to be elected. Edinburgh was at this time the only burgh in Scotland to enjoy the privilege of a member to itself. All the other burghs were represented by a single member sitting for four or five. The member for Edinburgh elected in 1780 was James Hunter Blair of Dunskey, a prosperous banker and a future Lord Provost of the city. He had been re-elected at the General Election of 1784 on 5 April, but in August he vacated the seat by applying for the Stewardship of the Manor of East Hendred and was now to be replaced.

The vacancy was due to a decision by Henry Dundas, till recently Lord Advocate and now a Privy Councillor, who was just reaching the peak of his unparalleled influence as political manager of Scotland for the Government. His decision was the incidental result of his desire to bring into Parliament Colonel Hugh Montgomerie of Skelmorlie, cousin and heir of the Earl of Eglinton. To allow him to sit for his native county of Ayrshire an alternative seat had to be found for the member who had held Ayrshire for ten years, Sir Adam Fergusson of Kilkerran. Being popular and respected as well as a friend of Dundas's, Sir Adam could not have been asked to withdraw in Montgomerie's favour without receiving the compensation of an alternative seat. Hunter Blair was either willing or persuaded to retire and Sir Adam was to be given the seat for Edinburgh—a gift it might be called, for Edinburgh was now firmly under Henry Dundas's control, the death of Sir Lawrence Dundas in 1781 having left him without a rival for its patronage and management.

Sir Adam moreover was well known in Edinburgh. He had been born and largely brought up there and a year before this he had been given the freedom of the city for his 'spirited and successfull efforts' in the House of Commons in defence of 'the interest and priviledges' of the University's Medical Department. The scheme to elect him had been adumbrated and was being talked of by well informed people in London within a month of Hunter Blair's election. There could be no obstacle to it. The only voters were the members of the Town Council and the Council, self-elected and self-perpetuating, was a comfortably harmonious body. The whole therefore was a simple arrangement, but the decencies of election had to be observed. 'Go into Edinburgh' was the advice of one of Sir Adam's oldest friends, an experienced burgh member, 'see the people, be known to them, and do all you can to make them believe you are their own choice.'

Sir Adam duly travelled from Ayrshire to Edinburgh, arriving on Tuesday 17 August. On Friday the *Edinburgh Advertiser* openly stated, 'We hear Sir Adam Fergusson is to be elected', a safe forecast which was repeated by the other papers next day and realized on Tuesday the 31st.

It was between this forecast and its fulfilment that James Tytler at last accompanied his balloon into the air and for the first and only time in his life enjoyed public esteem and praise.

5

The Grand Edinburgh Fire Balloon—II

Made cautious by the events of his failure on 10 August, Tytler had no wish for his next attempt, of the success of which he could not be certain, to be witnessed by a crowd. He therefore arranged it for an early hour in the morning of Wednesday 25 August, when the newly varnished balloon was raised and the fire beneath it lit at about a quarter past five.

None of the accounts of Tytler's balloon mention what fuel he used. Pilâtre de Rozier, as Tytler knew, had employed straw mingled with wisps of wool, and such fuel if Tytler followed his example would easily account for the smoke and also the sparks which had damaged the envelope previously. But since Tytler had resolved to try for the present an ascent without his stove the weight of the fuel was of no account and the fire on the ground could have been of wood or charcoal.

Whatever fed the fire on this occasion, a heat of 12 minutes sufficed to fill the balloon. But to make sure of drying it after its long exposure to the weather and the recent varnishing, the fire was kept up for another hour. It would then be about half-past six and a fair number of people would be about. The fire was extinguished. Tytler got into his basket and the balloon was released.

Nothing much happened. This might be called Tytler's first ascent for the balloon did leave the ground, but that was all it did. It 'fairly raised itself' according to the *Caledonian Mercury*, or as the *Courant* put it 'the balloon, together with the projector himself, and basket in which he sat, were fairly floated', but no more.

Tytler was disappointed, and ascribed this abortive ascent to the too early extinction of the fire. Perhaps a chilly morning had contributed to cool the balloon too quickly. Still, it had left the ground. He would try again. As the *Mercury* observed; 'The practicability of the scheme was evident; and there is little doubt that another experiment will put it in his power to retort on those who have ridiculed him in distress.'

The *Mercury* itself contributed to that ridicule in the same issue, printing some feeble verses headed 'The RISE and FALL of the EDINBURGH FIRE BALLOON anticipated' which imagined the flight of 'the huge machine' as ending by its being driven against a steeple and Tytler's being thrown into a horse-pond. Statements occasionally printed, such as that by Chambers, that Tytler's successful flight did end in a horse-pond or on a dunghill—completely untrue—may have had their foundation in this silly lampoon.

Tytler could afford to disregard it. Two days later—on Friday 27 August 1784—his balloon at last made its historic flight. In the *Dictionary of National Biography* the only contemporary authority for it quoted is the brief second-hand report in the *Gentleman's Magazine* which concluded on a note of doubt—'He *claims* the honour to be the first person who has navigated the air in Great Britain.' Yet the *Edinburgh Advertiser* and *Edinburgh Evening Courant* published accounts of the ascent the same evening and the *Caledonian Mercury* the following day. With these immediate reports and Tytler's own account written less than two years afterwards the whole event is well documented.

Once more Tytler fixed his attempt for an early hour, five o'clock. It was a fine, calm morning, with a very gentle breeze from the south-west. The balloon, 'new varnished and very tight', was hoisted up and the fire underneath kept burning strongly for nearly an hour until the balloon was well filled and pulling at its ropes with great force. Tytler felt certain that it was capable of lifting half a ton. The favourable moment had come at last. Once more he took his seat in the little basket and the securing ropes were released.

Up shot the balloon and its passenger, but only to be immediately checked, partly by a rope which was one of the stays of the mast and partly by the branches of a tree. Cleared of these obstructions it finally soared into the air.

The spectators raised a loud huzza. Tytler waved his hat. He rose to a height of 350 feet, as measured by a cord left hanging from the basket, and might have mounted higher but for the check at the balloon's release and the alarm of some of his people on the ground who caught hold of the trailing cord. But the balloon's strength was enough to tear it from their hands and the breeze wafted Tytler northwards over the slight rise of Abbey Hill and on for about half a mile from Comely Garden. Then as the air within the envelope cooled the balloon sank gently downwards and touched ground on the road to Restalrig.

It was undoubtedly a balloon flight, but too short for any observations of value even if Tytler had taken any instruments up with him, and not been too excited to think of anything but the enjoyment of his triumph. He said afterwards that he had amused himself with 'looking at the spectators running about in confusion below', that he found the sensation of flight most agreeable and had not felt any giddiness. He was in high spirits as he talked to the press reporters and already spoke of making a longer journey next time.

For once, during this August week-end, the indefatigable Tytler with his long record of fruitless ventures, with his dingy, untidy clothes and a hole in his hat, thriftless, improvident and disreputable, found himself taken seriously, hailed as a courageous pioneer and congratulated on the persistence which had at last brought him success. The Edinburgh papers did not at this time of his actual achievement underrate what he had accomplished. 'Mr Tytler', categorically declared the *Edinburgh Advertiser*, 'is the first person in Great Britain to have navigated the air.' The formerly unfriendly *Edinburgh Evening Courant* prefixed to its report of his feat a positive eulogy of Tytler, filled with excited alliteration: 'While we stand amazed at the boldness of the undertaking, we cannot at the same time sufficiently admire the patience and perseverance of the projector. . . . The scheme being in general looked upon as visionary or impracticable . . . he had not only public prejudice, but personal poverty, to struggle with.' And the *Caledonian Mercury* next day called the ascent 'a decisive experiment' and proclaimed, 'Scotland, as well as France, may boast of its aerial navigator'.

Public interest was now really aroused, and Tytler was pressed to give another exhibition of his balloon's capabilities. This time there could be no question of a discreet attempt in the early morning. Tytler must dare the full light of day and of publicity. No doubt scientific interest was voiced from the University. But there was also a report of 'the desire of several noblemen and gentlemen', who were gathered in Edinburgh at this time by the circumstances of the imminent by-election. This may have precipitated Tytler's taking what he later called 'another *leap*' for which he should really have made longer preparation.

The second flight took place four days later, on Tuesday 31 August. That forenoon the by-election was held in the Council Chamber. Mr Hunter Blair made a valedictory speech, 'very elegant and animated', and then, 'after the usual forms had been gone through, the Lord Provost proposed Sir Adam Fergusson as representative for this city: and the roll of the Council being called, Sir Adam was elected without a dissentient voice'.

The new member was sent for from the ante-chamber where he had been waiting and informed of his election. He thanked the Council for the honour they had done him, recalling his particular attachment to the city of Edinburgh in which he had drawn his first breath and had received his education. The *Courant* reported that he spoke with 'easy eloquence' and praised him as 'a man of candour, integrity and virtue', and the *Advertiser* observed that his election gave 'universal satisfaction', adding: 'The great attention of Sir Adam, when in Parliament, to the affairs of this country, and his exertions in favour of the Scots Universities, when a bill was brought in against them, will long be gratefully remembered.' He proved indeed an active and popular member for Edinburgh for the next five years, and gave early proof of his goodwill to the city four days after his election by a donation of £100 to its Charity Workhouse.

Meanwhile, as soon as his election was over, Sir Adam gave an 'elegant entertainment' to the Lord Provost, magistrates and principal citizens. This took place in the Assembly Hall in Buccleuch Street, and when the party had broken up the new Member of Parliament went down to Comely Garden to see the balloon about which everyone was talking. Presumably he had been one of the 'noblemen and gentlemen' who had since the previous Friday expressed their desire to witness its performance. The names of others as well as his were mentioned by the *Edinburgh Advertiser* as present on this day—the Marquis of Graham and Captain the Hon. Keith Stewart, a distinguished naval officer, both of them likewise members of the House of Commons. Major-General the Hon. Alexander Leslie, Lord Leven and Melville's brother, a veteran of the American Revolutionary War, was there too. So were some of the professors from the University who, though unnamed, perhaps included Tytler's former teacher Dr Cullen. Many ladies were also among the 'genteel company' assembled, including Lady Townshend, a noted beauty and a leader of fashion, who came of a Peeblesshire family, and the Hon. Mrs Montgomery, apparently her sister-in-law. All these had no doubt taken their places in Comely Garden; and besides those who had bought tickets for a close view of the balloon, crowds of people had gathered on the slopes of Arthur's Seat and the Calton Hill. Many more were nearer at hand, and so many of the populace pushed their way into the Garden that Tytler was 'much incommoded'.

He could not have hoped for a better audience nor more influential witnesses when he ordered the inflation of his balloon to begin at two o'clock in the afternoon. But the display with which he favoured them failed to rise to such an opportunity. The lifting power of the balloon on the 27th seems to have surprised him and made him a little apprehensive of what might happen if the wind, which was blowing lightly from the south, took charge of the balloon of which he had no sort of control. He stopped the inflation therefore after only half an hour, and ordered his men to check the balloon's upward spring on its release. None the less it 'overturned five or six people' as Tytler, seated in his basket, rose into the air to a height which the *Edinburgh Evening Courant* estimated as 100 feet, sailed over the Comely Garden pavilion, and 'descended gradually in a garden at a little distance on the other side'. Such was Tytler's second balloon ascent, or third if the attempt of 25 August be counted.

It was not a very striking performance. But being, like its predecessor, made without the stove, so that the balloon's bubble of hot air was cooling with every moment of its flight, it could not at the best have been more than a 'leap'. I have not been able to find that any of the distinguished assembly wrote an account of it. The *Edinburgh Advertiser* stated that 'it was intended merely to shew the practicability of the scheme, many gentlemen having, we hear, withheld their subscriptions on a supposition that the whole was a *humbug*, and that Mr Tytler never meant to go up. We understand that this bold and indefatigable *Aeronaut* purposes to make his grand aerial expedition, provided he receives subscriptions sufficient to enable him to complete his plan, by getting a stove, and other necessary appendages.'

There is some inconsistency in contemporary references to the financing of the balloon. The *Caledonian Mercury* reported that 'a great number of genteel company attended, who contributed pretty liberally for the projector'. The *Courant*, however, which considered this brief ascent of the 31st successful and promising, only expressed its hope that a subscription would be opened, and said that if everyone in the 'vast concourse of spectators, who were highly pleased . . . paid but the merest trifle, this ingenious and bold adventurer might have been enabled to complete his plan, and been rewarded for his trouble'.

5 Henry Dundas, c. 1785

4 Sir Adam Fergusson, Bart., 1786

It seems at any rate that Tytler did raise enough money to allow him to have a new stove and 'gallery' made, on the construction of which he spent most of September. At this time the Italian aeronaut Vincent Lunardi was preparing to make his much better organized and far more skilfully publicized balloon ascent in London on 15 September; and the balloon fever was at its height. In France the triumphs of the early aeronauts had inspired an extraordinary outburst of decorative art, and designers of furniture, clocks and porcelain were all commemorating them with charming variations on the allied curves of distended globe and pendent gondola. There were chairs 'à la montgolfière', gilded clocks 'au ballon', balloon designs in silk, in marquetry panels, or on cups and plates. Balloons appeared on watches, snuff-boxes, seals, buttons and ladies' fans. The vogue spread across the Channel but with somewhat less of elegance. 'Everything with us is à la ballon', wrote a London correspondent, the grammar being perhaps his own, early in September. Milliners were selling 'balloon hats', jewellers 'balloon earrings', greengrocers labelling ordinary pears as 'balloon pears'. Toyshops produced toy fire balloons of, so to speak, one candle power which sold freely. They could be seen floating in the mild autumn evenings in every part of London and were alleged to have started at least three serious fires. Meanwhile a model fire balloon 22 feet round was sent up in Perth which was seen 'passing over the village of Moulin' 24 miles away and later blown back almost to its starting-point. Though rainy weather delayed Tytler's next attempt for some time he could depend on continued public interest in aerostation.

At length he advertised Thursday 29 September as the date of his next flight. That morning proved calm but at about noon a gusty wind arose, from the east this time, and the conditions began to look hazardous. The balloon was hoisted half-way up its mast and partially filled with hot air. For three-quarters of an hour Tytler waited for some moderation of the wind. Then there was an accident. A pin by which the balloon was secured to the mast came out and the balloon slowly sank to earth and was narrowly prevented from catching fire as it settled down over the stove.

Tytler would at this point have abandoned the attempt for that day. But an immense crowd had gathered to see it in Comely Garden, in St Ann's Yards and on the Calton Hill and it was clear that they wanted the exhibition at whatever risk. After an interval of an hour or so the balloon was hoisted again, this time to the top of the mast. Here it felt the full force of the wind and the result was disastrous. The mast broke and everything fell to the ground with a crash. Two men were on the mast at the time. One was badly hurt by his fall; the other saved himself by catching at a tree and clinging to it.

All was over for this time and the discontented crowd melted away. 'Should any further attempt be made by Mr Tytler in this aerial project', observed the *Caledonian Mercury* that evening, 'we are persuaded he will never again be so well attended, as the chagrin occasioned by the present failure cannot fail of having disgusted many who were most sanguine in favour of the projector.' The *Courant* pointed out the by now obvious fact that a hot air balloon 'cannot possibly ascend but when there is almost a dead calm'; and the *Advertiser* rather acidly remarked: 'These aerial expeditions are only a matter of curiosity and speculation, not of practical utility, and the question always recurs—*Cui Bono*?'

But Tytler did not give up yet. He got a strong new mast from Leith and had it securely stayed. The balloon was repaired once more. He intended his next flight to be a real aerial journey, carrying at last the 'gallery' and stove which would maintain the heated air in the envelope and thus the buoyancy of the balloon.

A favourable day dawned on 11 October. It was as fine as could be wished, with hardly a breath of wind. Again there was a crowd of spectators, 'both respectable and numerous', and again they were disappointed. The balloon was filled by one o'clock and remained in that state, attached to its mast, till three. Tytler then got into the basket, the balloon was cast off—and nothing happened. The balloon, it appeared, could hardly support itself, much less lift its burden. Crestfallen, Tytler got out again. Then, in the words of the *Edinburgh Evening Courant*, 'the balloon, having rolled about a short time like an overgrown porpoise, at last rose slowly and heavily to the height of about a hundred yards, but being without any director, it fell sideways to the ground, nearly on the spot from which it rose; and thus end the travels and eventful history of the Edinburgh *Grand* Fire Balloon'.

From this account (followed verbatim by the *Edinburgh Advertiser*) and the *Caledonian Mercury*'s it would seem that the simple explanation of the fiasco is that Tytler had altogether miscalculated the lifting power that his balloon possessed when finally completed. He reckoned the total weight of himself, the stove and the 'gallery' to be 432 pounds. The *Edinburgh Evening Courant*, from what information other than Tytler's it is hard to guess, put the weight of 'Mr Tytler, with the machine and apparatus' at 968¼ pounds, which seems an incongruously high figure even if it was supposed to include the weight of the envelope and the cords.

In his exculpatory account of his balloon experiences written nearly two years later Tytler put forward two explanations of his failure. One was that the balloon was 'leaking at every pore' from the damage it had received on 29 September. This is a little hard to believe since it had been carefully examined and repaired since. The other was that the stove which he had ordered to be made three feet in diameter had without his knowledge been reduced to a diameter of two feet three inches and consequently could not generate enough heat. He had wanted, he said, to make a private trial before the public one, in which case he would have discovered what was wrong, and had not intended to make any flight on 11 October. But having received a message at about midday to come down to Comely Garden and found to his surprise more than a thousand people assembled there, he had felt forced to make the attempt for fear of being accused of cowardice. For the alteration of the stove and insistence on a flight without a trial Tytler blamed 'friends' and 'advisers' of whose identity there is no evidence.

These may be regarded as excuses evolved by the chagrined inventor when he afterwards looked back on this humiliating day. Nothing of them was reported in the newspapers at the time, to which he could have made any statement he chose. It is fairly certain that when he took his seat in his basket on 11 October he fully expected to rise and to be carried a long way on a real 'aerial voyage', for on the evidence of the *Edinburgh Evening Courant* he had equipped himself with a cork jacket.

The disappointment of the watching crowd was great. They saw the balloon struggle upwards but without its passenger. 'Some of the crowd on the Calton-hill indeed asserted, that he had got into the inside, and others swore that they saw him peeping out of the hole at the bottom.' The fickle newspapers which only six weeks before had hailed Tytler as a pioneer and praised his enterprise and perseverance now took upon themselves to accuse him of being a public nuisance. 'What a deal of time has been trifled away', scoffed the *Courant*, 'by the various exhibitions of this bungling and misshapen *smoke-bag*!' The *Advertiser* observed, 'However such exhibitions may gratify the idle and lounging part of society, it is [*sic*] attended with a very serious loss and inconvenience to people in business'; and the *Mercury*, after remarking that people would no longer be 'duped' into leaving their business to witness exhibitions of such uncertain success, inconsistently asked 'whether the Sheriff of the county, or other proper officer, should not put a negative on such imposition in future. It can have no good effect; and its tendency to promote idleness among the inferior ranks, who with one accord, desert their respective employments, is undoubted.'

'My situation', wrote Tytler afterwards, 'was miserable beyond description. I was obliged to hear my name called out wherever I went, to bear the insults of every black-guard boy, to hear myself called Cheat, Rascal, Coward and Scoundrel by those who had neither courage, honesty, nor honour. I was proscribed in the newspapers, and pointed out by two of the Edinburgh News-mongers as a public enemy.'

Still, by his own account, Tytler persisted. But hereafter the Edinburgh newspapers ignored him, and for the history of his last two attempts at balloon ascents, both unsuccessful, we are dependent on his own statements since neither was reported in the press. His narrative of the first of them is as follows.

'It was still in my power to get a new stove constructed, and as I might now make it of any form I pleased, without interruption from *advisers*, I resolved to err on the safe side, and made it three feet and a half in diameter. There was now no difficulty but from the bad state of the Balloon, which was become like a sieve, and no public experiment could be attempted. A day was set for a private one, but it proved so tempestuous that nothing could be done, and soon after the whole was arrested for damages, the greatest part of which had never been done by the Balloon or any one belonging to it. A law process ensued, which lasted six months; at the end of which I was cast. However, matters were compromised, and by means of a friend the Balloon was once more set at liberty.'

The statement about the law process is quite positive but cannot be substantiated, and this casts some doubt on Tytler's trustworthiness as a witness on his own behalf. Mr Williamson, the manager of Comely Garden, might well have claimed compensation for damage to his trees and perhaps also to the fences and gate from the irruption of the crowds on 7 and 27 August. But there is no evidence that he did. The records of the Burgh Court, the Sheriff Court and the Court of Session over this period contain no mention of any action whatever against James Tytler.

Undoubtedly however he was again in financial difficulties soon after the beginning of 1785. He must have exhausted whatever sum he had received by way of subscription towards his balloon project and he certainly fell again into debt, for on 18 March he was driven for the second time to take refuge in the debtors' sanctuary at Holyrood. This time the Register of Protections described him as 'James Tytler, chemist and baloon maker in Edinburgh', adding the note, 'Lodges in James Walker's, gardener'. There is no knowing how long he remained in Holyrood this time. It was presumably 'by means of a friend' that he regained his liberty.

The explanation of the 'law case' may simply be that Tytler used a grandiose term for his pecuniary difficulties during the winter of 1784-5 and that what drove him into sanctuary six months after the October fiasco was not a conviction for debt but a threat of prosecution for it, combined with a seizure of his balloon as a means of pressure on him. As with the friends who interfered with the design of the balloon's stove, a mist of anonymity veils the benefactor who arranged for Tytler's emergence from sanctuary, perhaps by the end of April, and for one more chance to demonstrate that his balloon could perform what he claimed for it.

'I could not immediately make any attempt', continues Tytler's narrative, 'by reason of a fever which confined me six weeks. No trial could be made in the former place, and it was difficult to procure another. The summer was spent in languid attempts to repair the Balloon.'

The balloon fever had not abated since Tytler's efforts of the previous summer and autumn. The *Scots Magazine* in its issue of November, under the heading 'AEROSTATION', remarked, 'Our readers may wish, in the present rage for balloons, to have a short and accurate account of the different aerostatic voyages which have been made since Mr Montgolfier's discovery', and then proceeded to list 28 'experiments', including Lunardi's ascent in London on 15 September and Sadler's on 4 October and 12 November but making no mention whatever of Tytler's. This was typical of the emphatic and deliberate ignoring of Tytler by the Edinburgh press after the beginning of September. The *Scots Magazine* indeed had never mentioned him at all.

Other balloon news had been duly reported—Sadler's flight from Oxford to Thame on 1 December, ascents by Blanchard, Godfrey (the first American aeronaut) and others, Lunardi's exhibition of a balloon 'one third larger than any yet constructed' and his plans for further ascents. Blanchard with a companion made the first crossing of the English Channel on 7 January 1785. A month later the Edinburgh Theatre Royal's advertisement of its production of *The Tempest* showed, like the fashionable Lunardi bonnet, how firmly anchored the balloon now was in the public taste. As altered by Dryden, *The Tempest, or The Inchanted Island* offered opportunities for extravagant fancy not to be missed, and the Theatre Royal production seized on them for a topical display. 'In the course of the Play will be introduced an AIR BALLOON . . . 1st, in its perpendicular ascent; and, 2dly, in its horizontal direction'—together with 'a distant view of Paris'.

The mere ascent of a real balloon could no longer impress the public and the task before Tytler was much more formidable than that of the previous year. Balloon voyages were becoming common, such as one made from Tottenham Court Road in London on 23 March. 'It was a most astonishing sight, the largest that has been sent up', wrote Lord Fife, an eyewitness. 'It went off charmingly and I kept sight of it till it appeared no larger than an egg. It is probably in Portsmouth, if not in the sea.' Actually it travelled only 35 miles, to Horsham in Sussex. Such voyages became commoner each month. On 5 May William Windham flew with Sadler over London, the first M.P. to take to the air, watched by Horace Walpole from Strawberry Hill.

To arouse any lively interest in 1785, Tytler would have to sail to Dundee or the Borders at least. His final attempt at a balloon flight was made, by his own account, on 26 July. Once more there is no confirmation to be found in contemporary newspapers but they do corroborate Tytler's attribution of this culminating disaster to violent weather, recording thunder and lightning, heavy showers of rain and even some hail on that day.

'At last', wrote Tytler, 'on the 26th of July an experiment was made. The place where it now was had a shelter only from the south and south-east winds. A fire was applied for four minutes, the wind blowing gently from the east. Some thunder was heard at a distance, and a vehement blast instantly followed from the south-west. The Balloon was torn from the hands of those who held it, several of them overturned, and their lives endangered; the stove was dashed in pieces, and the Balloon itself very much damaged. Soon after this, I abandoned the scheme and Edinburgh itself in despair.'

Where he now went is uncertain. His father died on 29 July at the age of 78 and Tytler may have visited his mother who would soon have to leave the manse of Fearn which had been her home for 40 years and who survived for a further ten. Tytler is said to have gone to Glasgow and there found employment with John Mennons, the printer who had produced for him the short-lived *Weekly Mirror*. Mennons had carried on business for many years in Edinburgh but commercial competition there was strong, and in 1783 he had had the enterprise to remove himself and his business to Glasgow and make a fresh start. There, provided only with a second-hand printing-press, some badly worn types and a capital of not more than £200, he had started a rival newspaper to the two already existing in Glasgow, the *Glasgow Advertiser*. It prospered for nearly 20 years before Mennons parted with his interest in it and it became the *Glasgow Herald and Advertiser*, later to develop into the still flourishing *Glasgow Herald*.

Tytler may well have earned a subsistence for a while as a contributor to the *Advertiser*. Writing had again become his only means of livelihood, though now and for many years he was known as Balloon Tytler. The nickname was all that remained of his most spectacular enterprise. Two months after his last failure his reputation as a balloonist was conclusively extinguished by the Italian Vincent Lunardi. Lunardi, arriving fresh from his triumphs in England, made a strikingly successful ascent on 5 October 1785 from the green before Heriot's Hospital on the south side of Edinburgh, achieving the 'aerial voyage' which Tytler had never been able to perform. The wind carried him over Edinburgh and as far east as North Berwick, and then shifting took him across the Firth of Forth to Fife where he descended safely near the village of Ceres. He made four other balloon flights in Scotland, all variously successful, before the end of the year.

Lunardi was a handsome young man—as he very well knew—of an ebullient and romantic temperament. He thoroughly understood the theatrical value of his performances which he exploited to the full, wearing a coat of scarlet with blue facings and waving a flag to the watching multitudes. Apparently he met Tytler, either in Edinburgh or in Glasgow, and treated him with sympathy and kindness. In the book which he published in 1786, *An Account of Five Aerial Voyages in Scotland*, dedicated to the Duke and Duchess of Buccleuch, he made generous reference to him in his characteristically flowery style:

'Before *my* arrival in Scotland several attempts had been made to launch a large FIRE BALLOON, but all without success. The poor man who should have gone up, how I commiserate his situation! Judge of his sensibility and misfortunes by the enclosed papers.' (Lunardi's book is in the form of letters to a friend.) 'I have seen the man', Lunardi goes on; 'I have offered the voice of consolation to aleviate [*sic*] his distresses; and dictates of humanity have been obeyed as far as lay in my power.'

Whether Lunardi consoled Tytler with money as well as kind words or not, Tytler was grateful for his friendliness and responded with a long and typically clumsy poem—'To Mr Lunardi, on his successful aerial voyages from Edinburgh, Kelso, and Glasgow. By J. Tytler.' In it he paid tribute to Lunardi's achievements which he represented as having comforted him for his own failures. The flattered Lunardi printed the whole thing in his book together with the long footnote, extending to more than four pages, which Tytler appended to the couplet

> *Lost are my wishes, lost is all my care,*
> *And all my projects flutter in the air.*

This note, not improbably the *raison d'être* of the poem, gives

Tytler's own account of his experiments and misfortunes which has been drawn upon in this and the preceding chapter.

It was the only chance that he found to put on record his conviction that misfortune and not miscalculation had been to blame for his balloon's failure. Too little is known, and that too imprecise, of its design, dimensions, composition and method of control for judgment of whether it ever could, given all favourable circumstances, have made a real 'voyage'. It never, after all, rose even once with the stove that might have maintained it in the air. But Tytler would admit only its bad luck. 'Such a series of disasters', he concluded, 'is almost unparalleled; but I pay myself too high a compliment in supposing that Heaven has declared war against me: the whole are easily deducible from want of *power* in myself, want of *knowledge* in my friends, and the *impatience* of the public in general.'

Not only the public's impatience but its almost constant attitude of contempt towards Tytler's project is perplexing, as too is that of the Edinburgh press. Only after his two ascents in August 1784 did the newspapers treat it with the seriousness it deserved. Before that time they gave him little encouragement and after it no sympathy. It may be presumed that the ordinary people of Edinburgh, except his few friends, treated him in the same way.

For the coldness and unkindness shown to him, his disreputable appearance, dubious associates and lack, probably, of anything impressive in his air or conversation do not altogether account. His own behaviour may have been partly responsible. Though of a kindly and sociable temperament he was extremely touchy. 'He had a keen perception', says Meek, 'of the slightest neglect or personal insult, and so completely qualified was he to punish it with his pen, that no one who knew him would have been solicitous to incur his displeasure.' He may have retorted against such slights as the snubbing paragraphs in the *Edinburgh Evening Courant* or the foolish lampoon in the *Caledonian Mercury* with unforgivable venom. If so, he was not the only inventor to make the mistake of antagonising the press. Moreover when, after his October failure, people insulted him in the streets of Edinburgh with the epithets of 'cheat, rascal, coward and scoundrel', Tytler probably gave as good as he got. If his behaviour was waspish when he was annoyed it is perhaps not altogether remarkable that his inability to perform what he had publicly promised aroused more satisfaction than sympathy.

Yet there is no doubt that, as the *Edinburgh Advertiser* had put it, he was 'the first person in Great Britain to have navigated the air', and serious histories of aviation give him, however briefly, that credit. Unfortunately his one really public ascent of only 100 feet was unimpressive, the word 'navigated' could hardly be applied to it, and Sir Adam Fergusson, General Leslie and the university professors who witnessed it could not be blamed if they dismissed Tytler's balloon as no more than a cumbrous toy of little scientific interest and no practical future that they could foresee.

As time went on the people of Edinburgh, many of whom had gaped at Lunardi's brilliant and spectacular balloon flight, forgot Tytler's brief success and remembered only his failures. Balloon Tytler was regarded not as the man who had ascended in a balloon but as the man who had tried but not succeeded. Chambers was misled by one of them. 'Old Alister Campbell', he wrote half a century after Tytler's death, 'who remembered the affair, described it to me a great many years ago in brief terms: "Tytler's balloon", said he, "rose over a dyke, and then quietly settled on a midden."' The balloon may in fact have landed on a midden in the garden where its second flight ended; but that was not all it did.

Nevertheless to land in a midden seemed appropriate to J. Tytler. 'It was a type', Chambers commented, 'of most of his ventures in life.' And so this contemptuous judgement of what was felt to be dramatically suitable to poor Tytler, the shabby and ridiculous drudge and dreamer, superseded recognition of his courage, his perseverance, and his indubitable achievement.

6

Tytler and Burns

For how long Tytler fled from Edinburgh after the final failure of his balloon is uncertain. He was probably still in Glasgow in 1786 when a new paper appeared called *The Observer* which ran for 26 issues and of which he is said to have written the first number, but he was in all likelihood back in Edinburgh before the end of that year.

The city was growing fast and many improvements could be seen. Cartloads of earth and rubbish from the foundations of the houses rising in the New Town were being piled in the valley south of Princes Street to form the 'Earthen Mound' which was soon to become a principal access from the Old Town to the New. The City Guardhouse had been removed from the middle of the High Street. Further east the South Bridge was being rapidly built to extend the roadway from the North Bridge over the Cowgate, although Robert Adam's magnificent scheme for its flanking buildings had run into difficulties which were to prevent its realization. Plans were beginning to be discussed for a new University building; and work had been resumed towards the completion of the Register House.

Tytler had to live by his pen, and the flourishing capital was though not the only place the best in which to find employment for it. In 1786 work began on a third edition of the *Encyclopaedia Britannica* which offered him another chance of regular earning. But his main means of livelihood was the old one: hack work at editing, abridging, translating, knocking other men's writing into new shapes for low and irregular pay, anonymous and unknown but to those who employed him. He may also have found occasional work as a printer; and if Anderson is right he continued somehow to dabble in chemical experiments, though how he found the means to do so is hard to imagine.

The children of his marriage to Elizabeth Rattray, if they had survived, were by now old enough to have found work and were perhaps no burden on him, but he was not free from domestic cares. By now he was living with Jean Aitkenhead, whose predecessor had died in childbed in 1782, and his miscellaneous family had been increased by the twin daughters whom Jean had borne to him. Paterson quotes a note on them left by Kay that at the age of four these two little girls were 'so remarkably like each other, that they were hardly to be distinguished from each other, even by their parents, who are often obliged to ask their name, individually, at the infants themselves'.

He was probably living once more in the city rather than in one of the outlying villages, haunting the doors of printers and book-sellers who might give him work, and haunting also the taverns where he certainly spent too much of his time. Not that drink ever impaired his faculty for work. Meek tells a vivid story in proof of this, though with no indication of which period of Tytler's life it concerns. An Edinburgh bookseller (Meek's informant) who knew Tytler's gift for rapid composition applied to him in an emergency for 'as much matter as would form a junction between a certain history and its continuation'. He called on Tytler late one evening and was told by his old landlady that he had gone to bed drunk. Insisting on seeing him, the bookseller climbed the stairs to the garret which Tytler occupied and with a lamp entered the room. Tytler was indeed drunk and in bed; but the bookseller, who must have been desperate for his copy, aroused him and stated his business. He got what he wanted. 'Mr Tytler called for paper, pen and ink, and in a short time produced about a page and a half of letter press, which answered the end proposed as completely as if it had been the result of the most mature deliberation, previous notice, and a mind undisturbed by the fumes of any liquor capable of deranging his ideas.'

In his sober moments Tytler had, either at this time or soon afterwards, a chance to maintain himself and his family by employment as a contributor to the third edition of the *Encyclopaedia Britannica*. The 1500 copies of the second edition of which he had been the chief compiler sold out in ten months, and Macfarquhar and Bell determined to undertake another and yet larger one. It would be understandable if Tytler declined to act as editor again but they may not have invited him. Macfarquhar himself took on the appointment and when he tired of it it was entrusted to an Episcopalian clergyman, Mr George Gleig. But Tytler was engaged as an established contributor to the new edition—'upon more liberal terms', says Anderson, than the partners had allowed him before—and wrote several important articles including, according to Meek, the one on Electricity.

The new edition took more than ten years to produce. It was extended to 18 volumes and a printing of 10,000 copies. Bell and Macfarquhar are said to have cleared from this edition alone a net profit of £42,000, though since Macfarquhar died before it was finished most of this must have gone to Bell. Even the 'corrector of the press' and the warehouseman did handsomely for themselves by procuring subscriptions for copies. But Tytler did not share in this profit, and long before the publication was completed he had left Scotland.

About this time he made the acquaintance of Robert Anderson, who had settled in Edinburgh in 1784. On this acquaintance was based Anderson's short but valuable account of Tytler's life and career. The warmth and sympathy of its tone show that a real friendship grew up between them, to which there is also testimony in the only two letters of Tytler's that I have been able to discover, both of which are addressed to Anderson but neither unfortunately bears a date. The following one, which for several reasons is worth giving in full, appears to have been sent while Tytler was writing

94

contributions to the *Encyclopaedia* and indirectly supports Meek's attribution to him of the article on Electricity. The bearer of the letter, 'D. Oliphant', was the bookseller who had undertaken the sale of Tytler's *General History of All Nations*, and was perhaps one of the nameless 'friends' who had both encouraged and embarrassed him in his balloon experiments.

Dear Sir

Since I saw you, I have been near the gates of death. I have had a dreadful attack of a malignant fever, the particulars of which I hope to relate to you on some future occasion. The disease was attacked on the Brunonian plan, and in the most *Herculean* manner. I became totally delirious on the third day, and continued so to the 7th.—I beg you will give the bearer D. Oliphant all the books I left in your house, including the half vol. of Encyc: Britannica, & particularly the System of Electricity which last I beg you will cause him wrap up in a bit of paper by itself, lest some of the loose leaves should be lost. This is the 14th day since I became ill and I am now eating to my breakfast—What?—Beef-stakes unalloyed even with bread. *O rare Bruno*!

I am Dear Sir

Yours most sincerely

JA. TYTLER.

Doctor Robert Anderson.

'Bruno' is a reference to Dr James Brown, ten years older than Tytler, who died in 1788. The Brunonian system of medicine which he founded was based on the then novel theory that most diseases were due to a debility of the system and should therefore be treated not in the time-honoured way by bleeding and a lowering diet but by measures of support and nourishment. Tytler had probably read his *Short Account of the Old Method of Cure, and Outlines of the New Doctrine*, published in 1786, but he was quite capable of having read earlier the Latin treatise, *Elementa Medicinae*, in which Brown had first set forth his ideas in 1780. This letter shows at the least that

95

he kept his medical knowledge up to date. It shows too that he possessed at any rate some books, though possibly not his own property. His only other surviving letter to Anderson, likewise undated, is a brief note asking for the loan of a Latin dictionary, which implied that he did not possess even such an essential working tool.

That he had left books at Anderson's house suggests that he must have been a guest there. Certainly Anderson, very likely as Tytler's host, saw one side of him which he is the only writer to record:

'Amidst the drudgery of writing, and the cares which pressed upon him daily, he exhilarated his spirits, at intervals, with a tune on the Irish Bagpipe, which he played with much sweetness, interposing occasionally a song of his own composition, sung with great animation. A solace of this kind was well suited to the simplicity of his manners, the modesty of his disposition, and the integrity of his character, such as they were before he suffered his social propensities to violate the rules of sobriety.'

The animation with which Tytler would give 'a song of his own composition' may have made its deficiencies less noticeable. But indeed his songs were as undistinguished as his formal poems. None the less it was the fact that he sometimes wrote songs that brought him to the notice of that tireless collector and restorer of the folksongs of Scotland, Robert Burns.

It was in November 1786, in the first flowering of his renown as a poet, that Burns rode into Edinburgh on a borrowed pony, committed to the project of arranging to publish a new edition of the poems which he had had printed at Kilmarnock in July with such resounding success. He remained there till the following May, his new edition being published on 21 April. During this successful visit to the capital he met, among the members of the convivial club known as the Crochallan Fencibles, the music-publisher James Johnson who issued in May the first volume of a new venture, *The Scots Musical Museum*. This was planned to be a collection of Scots songs old and new, and Burns became an enthusiastic contributor to the second and subsequent volumes.

It may have been during this stay in Edinburgh that Burns came across Tytler but it may not have been till his later visit in the winter of 1787-8, for the first allusion to Tytler in Burns's correspondence does not occur till 13 November 1788, in a letter to his Ayrshire friend Mrs Dunlop of Dunlop. Explaining the authorship of some of the songs in Johnson's second volume, Burns remarked, 'Those marked, T, are the work of an obscure, tippling though extraordinary body of the name of Tytler: a mortal, who though he drudges about Edinburgh as a common printer, with leaky shoes, a sky-lighted hat, and knee-buckles as unlike as George-by-the-grace-of-God, and Solomon-the-son-of-David, yet that same unknown drunken mortal is author and compiler of three fourths of Elliot's pompous Encyclopedia Brittanica.'

In fact only one of the songs in the volume is marked T. Its authorship is further attested by a note in Burns's hand in his own interleaved copy of the *Scots Musical Museum*—'This Song is the composition of Balloon Tytler.' But Burns's thumbnail sketch of its author is of the greatest biographical value. It is the only known written impression of Tytler's appearance, and bears out Meek's charitable understatement that 'he was far from paying much attention to dress'. It reflects the general public attitude towards Tytler, half pity and half contempt, and confirms his established reputation for 'tippling'. But it also demonstrates that his extraordinary labours on the second edition of the *Encyclopaedia Britannica*—credited by Burns to one of the associated printers named on its title-page—were despite their anonymity a matter of common knowledge in Edinburgh. Yet it shows too how little fame his balloon ascents had gained him, a nickname but no more. Only four years after his efforts in Comely Garden the *Encyclopaedia* was remembered but the Grand Edinburgh Fire Balloon was forgotten.

The song in the *Scots Musical Museum* marked T is a dreary one with an equally dreary tune, entitled 'The Young Man's Dream'.

97

Like Tytler's more formal verses it shows absolutely no originality and is merely a patchwork of the rags and tatters of conventional pastoral lyric. It begins:

> *One night I dream'd I lay most easy*
> *By a murm'ring river's side,*
> *Where lovely banks were spread with daisies,*
> *And the streams did smoothly glide,*
> *While all around me and quite over,*
> *Spreading branches were display'd,*
> *All interwoven in due order*
> *Soon became a pleasant shade.*
>
> *I saw my lass come in most charming*
> *With a look and air so sweet;*
> *Ev'ry grace was most alarming,*
> *Ev'ry beauty quite complete.*
> *Cupid with his bow attended;*
> *Lovely Venus too was there;*
> *As his bow young Cupid bended,*
> *Far away fled carking care.*

Another half-dozen stanzas describe how the lover tried to steal a kiss, how the lass was angry and struck down Cupid's bow, and how Cupid in revenge summoned Care and 'destructive Time' to wreck her beauty. Lovely Venus, whose presence the poet seems to have forgotten, made no intervention. The poem depressingly concludes:

> *As her charms were swift decaying,*
> *And the furrows seiz'd her cheek,*
> *Forbear, ye fiends! I vainly crying*
> *Wak'd in the attempt to speak.*

Another and very different song in the *Museum*—'I hae laid a herrin in saut'—on which Burns commented 'I like it much' has been ascribed to Tytler by Chambers. It is a pleasant and amusing song in which an earnestly practical lover details all the provision he has laid in in his 'house on yonder muir' with a view to marriage and presses his lass for her answer with the refrain 'And I canna come ilka day to woo'. It is too neatly and happily turned to credit to Tytler and indeed no one but Chambers has thought of doing so. Burns made no note on the authorship of the song in his interleaved copy of the *Museum*.

But Burns is again the authority for Tytler's responsibility for another song which had some popularity, probably on account of its tune—'The bonny brucket[1] lassie', which had appeared in the *Museum*'s first volume. In 1793, when there was a question of re-printing this song in *A Select Collection of Original Scotish Airs*, Burns wrote to the publisher George Thomson, 'The verses of "The bonny brucket lassie" are poor. They, I believe, are the production of that odd being, Balloon Tytler. The air deserves fine verses.'

Tytler's five stanzas are put into the mouth of a betrayed girl left pregnant by a lover who returns at the conclusion with a pro-mise to prove faithful after all. The first runs

> *The bonny brucket lassie,*
> *She's blue beneath the een;*
> *She was the fairest lassie*
> *That danced on the green.*
> *A lad he lo'ed her dearly,*
> *She did his love return;*
> *But he his vows has broken,*
> *And left her for to mourn.*

This seems to be based on a folk-song, for there is something of the ring of one in the opening and Cromek ascribes to Burns the opinion that 'the first two lines are all of it that is old'. But the rest is commonplace, with Tytler's characteristic touch of bathos—

---

[1] Tear-streaked.

My person it was comely,
My shape they said was neat;
But now I am quite changed,
My stays they winna meet.

Burns's judgment of the song as 'poor' was as sound as it usually was. None the less Cromek thought 'The bonny brucket lassie' worth reprinting in his *Select Scotish Songs* in 1810.

Another song in the first volume of the *Scots Musical Museum* is identified by Chambers as Tytler's with much more probability and is certainly in his manner—'Loch Eroch Side'. For the well-known old dance tune to which it had been set Burns provided new verses, 'Young Peggy blooms our bonniest lass', not one of his best efforts though he got Johnson to print it in a later volume of the *Museum*. But the tune has become better known as that of Lady Nairne's song 'The Lass o' Gowrie'. Loch Eroch is Loch Ericht on the borders of Perthshire and Inverness-shire.

Tytler's three verses, beginning

As I came by Loch Eroch side,
The lofty hills surveying,

and telling, of course, how

I met, unsought, my lovely maid,

are not quite so clumsy as usual but absolutely conventional. Once more the Muses to whom he paid court turned a deaf ear, as the conclusion shows:

Enraptured then, My lovely lass,
I cried, no more we'll tarry;
We'll leave the fair Loch Eroch side,
For lovers soon should marry.

Finally, one more song in the *Scots Musical Museum*, 'The Mucking of Geordie's Byre' (the last word spelt 'byar' throughout the *Museum* text) was ascribed to Tytler half a century after his death by another editor, William Stenhouse, in his collection *Illustrations of the Lyric Poetry and Music of Scotland*. Both words and air are quite different from those of a well-known song of the same name. If this homely and unaffected ditty about a girl who has married beneath her but not repented it is really Tytler's, as from one or two awkward touches in it seems quite likely, it is far the best of his identifiable songs and the only one worth giving in full. Like 'The bonny brucket lassie' it is based on an earlier original, and two lines, says Stenhouse, are 'taken from the old chorus'.

> *As I went over yon meadow,*
>   *And carelessly passed along,*
> *I listen'd with pleasure to Jenny,*
>   *While mournfully singing this song.*
> *The mucking of Geordie's byre,*
>   *And the shooling*[1] *the graip*[2] *so clean,*
> *Has aft gart*[3] *me spend the night sleepless,*
>   *And brought the salt tears in my een.*
>
> *It was not my father's pleasure,*
>   *Nor was it my mother's desire*
> *That ever I puddl'd my fingers*
>   *Wi' the mucking o' Geordie's byre.*
> *The mucking &c.*
>
> *Though the roads were ever so filthy,*
>   *Or the day so scoury*[4] *and foul,*
> *I wald ay be ganging wi' Geordie;*
>   *I lik'd it far better than school.*
> *The mucking &c.*

[1] Shovelling.
[2] Dung-fork.
[3] Caused.
[4] Showery, stormy.

My brither abuses me daily
For being wi' Geordie so free,
My sister she ca's me hoodwinked,
Because he's below my degree.
The mucking &c.

But well do I like my young Geordie,
Altho' he was cunning and slee;
He ca's me his Dear and his Honey,
And I'm sure that my Geordie lo'es me.
The mucking &c.

At about the time that Tytler came under Burn's notice in Edinburgh he was at work on yet another compendium of knowledge which was published in the course of 1788. Tytler's authorship is vouched for by Anderson but he is not named on the title-page except as 'the author of the continuation of Salmon's Geographical Grammar'.

Thomas Salmon was a laborious author of an earlier generation who produced many works, chiefly historical, of the scissors-and-paste kind, and his *New Geographical and Historical Grammar* was a well-known text-book published in 1749 but never revised and by now long out of date. I have not managed to trace Tytler's 'continuation' of it. But he was quite ready to tackle the voluminous Salmon on his own ground with a book of nearly 400 octavo pages of miscellaneous information of which the contents were thus summarized in its title:

'A NEW AND CONCISE System of Geography; CONTAINING A PARTICULAR ACCOUNT OF THE EMPIRES, KINGDOMS, STATES, PROVINCES, and ISLANDS, IN THE KNOWN WORLD. In which is included a Comprehensive History of Remarkable and Interesting Events. WITH AN INTRODUCTION, Exhibiting the Principles of Astronomy, as they are connected with the Knowledge of GEOGRAPHY.'

The book was further 'embellished with a set of accurate maps

engraved purposely for the work'. The preface drew attention to
the fact that the 'Comprehensive History' included a sketch of the
history of Scotland 'especially with respect to the Highlands and
Western Isles'. Tytler had no personal knowledge of this region but
his emphasis on it shows his awareness that with the recent foundation of the Highland Society and the British Fisheries Society public
interest in it was aroused and information about it could expect a
welcome.

The book as a whole was as superficial as its ambitious scope
suggests it was bound to be. It is worth noting however that on
pages 69–70 Tytler again drew on his early experiences for an account
of the method of harpooning whales.

Another compilation of Tytler's which must have been nearly as
laborious in research did not reach publication. It was a collection
called *The Universal Voyager and Traveller*, and was designed to
assemble all the navigational details of the famous voyages of
exploration. Tytler brought it down to the time of Anson but did
not manage to finish it. Meek says that he 'perused part of the
manuscript' which in 1805 was still 'in the possession of a gentleman
in Edinburgh', presumably one of the booksellers. But he says
nothing to indicate whether it was an early work abandoned for lack
of encouragement or one of the tasks that Tytler had in hand when
he was obliged to leave Scotland.

The *System of Geography* was 'printed for Peter Hill, at Thomson's
Head, Parliament Square'. It was one of Hill's very first publications,
for he had only in this year set up as an independent bookseller,
having previously been assistant to William Creech, a highly prosperous bookseller and himself an author. Creech was now one of the
bailies of Edinburgh and was later to become its Provost. It was he
who had published the first Edinburgh edition of Burns's poems.
Peter Hill, who had had a good deal to do with getting that book
through the press, became one of Burns's best friends and corres-
pondents in Edinburgh.

Conceivably it was in Hill's company that Burns saw Tytler,

took note of his odd appearance and learnt of his incongruous literary reputation. But they had another common acquaintance in Dr Robert Anderson. Anderson has the distinction of having been the very first critic to review Burns's Kilmarnock volume, his notice of which had appeared in the *Edinburgh Magazine* at the end of October 1786 and, despite a few criticisms, had hailed the unknown poet with praise and admiration, for Anderson's immediate reaction when he first perused his book had been, as he afterwards recalled, 'wonder and delight'.

This favourable review had been one of the factors which turned Burns from his plan to emigrate to the West Indies and determined him to try his fortune with a second edition of his poems in Edinburgh. Soon after he arrived there Anderson met him at a dinner-party given for him by the printer of the *Edinburgh Evening Courant*. 'We immediately entered into conversation', he later wrote, 'and in five minutes conversed as familiarly as if we had been acquainted five years'. During the winter of 1786–7 Anderson saw Burns frequently and had long talks with him on his reading, his opinions and the sources of his inspiration. But after Burns moved to Dumfriesshire they never met again.

Since Anderson was thus well acquainted with both Burns and Tytler he could easily have brought them together. Yet Burns's description of Tytler to Mrs Dunlop does not give the impression that they had in fact met. Rather it suggests that Tytler had been pointed out and described to Burns when casually noticed from a window as he shuffled along the street. It is quite likely that neither Anderson nor Hill wanted actually to introduce to Burns so disreputable a figure as that which he recalled in 1788.

7

Divorce and Flight

During the next few years after Tytler's balloon experiments it is to be presumed that he supported himself, Jean Aitkenhead and their twin daughters in his old way by undertaking such work as he could get from the booksellers, and principally by his contributions to the third edition of the *Encyclopaedia Britannica*. But his busy mind could not be restricted to hack work of this sort. 'It was his misfortune', says Anderson, 'to be continually drawn aside from the business of his employers by the delight he took in prosecuting experiments in chemistry, electricity, and mechanics, which consumed a large portion of his time and money.'

Though writing was his means of livelihood the examples of it already quoted will make it clear enough that he had no gift for literature. With a moderate independence, or even with some discerning patron to direct him, he would probably have found a career in some form of industry, for scientific experiment seems to have been his real interest and 'chemist' was the term by which he was almost invariably described. Given the chance, and had he possessed or somehow acquired the steadiness of character which he lacked, he might even have made a name for himself among the early pioneers of the industrial revolution in Scotland. Unfortunately, while his worthless literary labours can be hunted down in libraries, there is no record of his scientific experiments, evidence of which rests on the vaguest allusions only.

It was not only his home-made printing-press and the unlucky affair of the Grand Edinburgh Fire Balloon that gave testimony of his inventiveness. Kay's notes quoted by Paterson, clearly (from the allusion to the age of Jean's twins) made in about 1787, mention two of the pursuits which Anderson had in mind as consuming Tytler's time and money. One was a dream as seductive as the quest of mediaeval alchemists for the philosopher's stone 'which turneth all to gold'. 'He is at present engaged', wrote Kay, 'in the construction of a machine which, if he completes it according to his expectations, will in all probability make his fortune . . . the *perpetuum mobile*, or an instrument which, when once set agoing, will continue in motion for ever.' The other was much more practical—'He has just completed a chemical discovery of a certain water for bleaching linen, which performs the operation in a few hours, without hurting the cloth.' This might indeed have proved highly profitable, but probably, as with the balloon, there was some fatal flaw or oversight which doomed its failure.

Another invention, vouched for by both Anderson and Meek, did bring success, but not to Tytler. This was a method of preparing magnesia, from which Tytler failed to benefit on account, it would seem, of his unbusinesslike nature whenever he had to conclude any commercial agreement. The allusions of both biographers are extremely vague, but it seems that Tytler was cheated by his partner, one Robert Wright, who carried on the manufacture at Colinton, a village lying in a romantic wooded valley four miles south-west of Edinburgh. Wright apparently supplied the capital for the process and Tytler the idea. 'But after he had disclosed his secret to the gentleman at whose expence it was carried on, he was dismissed, without obtaining either a share in the business, or a suitable compensation for his services.'

Possibly Tytler shifted his home to Colinton for a while during the period of this partnership, for 'Collington, Monday morning' is the date of one of his two surviving letters to Dr Anderson already mentioned, which runs thus:

Dear Sir
   If you can spare me a Latin Dictionary per Bearer it will be a

favour, as I have got something to translate into that language. I will
return the Book to-morrow, as I am to come into town myself, and
must have the Job done before I come in. I am

Dear Sir

Your obliged friend

Doctor Robt. Anderson.   JA. TYTLER.

An unknown hand has endorsed this note, 'To Dr Anderson from
Mr James Tytler a most ingenious but eccentric and unfortunate
author'.

Leith—Duddingston—Restalrig—Colinton: all were within the
environs of Edinburgh which formed the scene of almost all Tytler's
labours and struggles until he left Scotland, though it is only occasionally that there are hints of where precisely he lived in or about
the city during the 21 years between his return thither in 1772 and
his flight in 1793. And twice at least during those years he left it:
once, by his own account, in 1785 after his final humiliation as a
balloonist, and again, in the early spring of 1788, in the course of a
new chapter of troubles, the beginning of which must have been
wholly unexpected.

It was more than a dozen years since his marriage to Elizabeth
Rattray had foundered. They had gone their separate ways and
Elizabeth, after remaining for a while in Edinburgh, had departed to
Orkney. The separation was total but they were still married. Of
this fact Tytler was suddenly and disagreeably reminded when early
in 1788 Elizabeth faced him with an action for divorce.

Nothing being known of her character and circumstances, her
motives for this action so long after her breach with her husband
can only be guessed. Perhaps she had found an opportunity of
marrying again, being now possibly not more than 40.

She was at this time living at Rackwick in the island of Hoy. The
only conceivable explanation for her having found so distant and
improbable a home on departing from Edinburgh is that she had

relations there. A remoter, wilder or more barren spot can hardly be imagined. Rackwick was a tiny community, a township planted on the shore where a valley stretched down to the Atlantic between stupendous precipices of sandstone rock, set in some of the most awful and magnificent scenery in the whole of the British Isles. The bay faced the western end of the Pentland Firth and the Atlantic billows crashed upon its shore, sometimes flinging there the bodies of drowned sailors for the folk of Rackwick to bury, sometimes carrying away the sheep which varied their pasture by browsing on the seaweed. The sheep, which ran wild, some poor oats and barley, and potatoes were the people's only sustenance, and peat their only fuel. In the whole mountainous island of Hoy there were not 300 inhabitants, who formed a pitiably poor community, as neglected as they were frugal. Their aged minister—he had entered on the charge three years before Tytler's father came to Fearn—lived in a ruinous and decaying manse and the parish church had just fallen down.

To start a legal action from Rackwick was an enterprise in itself. Elizabeth would be obliged to sail round the north end of the island, passing the Old Man of Hoy and St John's Head, or else take the steep five-mile walk up the valley and across to the little kirkton on the north-east shore and find a boat there. In any case she must cross Hoy Sound to reach the small town of Stromness on the Mainland of Orkney and consult one of the two writers (solicitors) who practised there. He in turn would have to correspond with one in Edinburgh, so that any matter needing discussion by letter might take many weeks to formulate.

In the light of all this, Elizabeth probably started her action in the late summer or early autumn of 1787. Eventually Mr Anthony Woodhead, writer in Forrester's Wynd, Edinburgh, took it in hand and on 23 January 1788 a formal summons of divorce was issued against 'James Tytler, sometime druggist in Leith, now chymist at or near Edinburgh'. It was executed on the 26th. The messenger, failing to apprehend Tytler personally, was obliged to leave the document at his dwelling-house—wherever that was at this time.

The summons narrated Elizabeth's version of the marriage and its failure. 'Without any cause the said James Tytler totally withdrew his affection from the said complainer his spouse and obliged her to leave his house' and soon afterwards 'took up with another woman of the name of Cairns with whom he cohabited under the title or appellation of his wife for severall years and by her he had one or two children, and she having died in childbed as is said, he the said James Tytler drew up with Jean Aitkenhead . . . who he also calls his wife and is now living and cohabiting with her as such, and has had twin children by her. From all which it is manifestly evident that the said James Tytler defender has been guilty of the crime of adultery.'

Cited to appear on 20 February in the Commissary Court of Edinburgh in answer to this summons, Tytler lodged defences on the 28th through a solicitor named John Wood. His adultery being indeed 'manifestly evident' it may seem strange that he should have contested the action, but his wife's claim for damages would be motive enough. Elizabeth was demanding all her privileges that she could have if she were his widow, £50 in damages and her legal expenses. The last item, considering the awkwardness of communication between Stromness and Edinburgh, might well be considerable; and £50 would be as hard for Tytler to raise in Edinburgh as it would seem wealth in Rackwick. Divorce to Tytler would spell ruin, or another retirement into Holyrood.

But since he could neither deny nor explain away his association with Jean Aitkenhead and the twins, he had no possible defence but to find legal flaws in Elizabeth's case. Mr Wood did what he could to this end. The copy of the summons served on Tytler had a blank where Jean Aitkenhead's name should have been; and Elizabeth Rattray though named was not designated. The defence therefore asked the Court to 'dismiss the action as irregularly brought' and find Tytler entitled to his full expenses.

So flimsy a defence did not encourage Tytler to remain to see its effect. He felt it prudent, as he had done in 1766, to retire into

England, but he went no further than was necessary to put himself beyond the Court's jurisdiction, to Berwick-upon-Tweed. From there on 3 March he dated a mandate to Mr John Wood to conduct his defence, and appointed Mr Wood's house in Edinburgh 'as my Domicile, where all summonses and other Necessary Papers relative to the said Action may be left for me during its dependence'.

The mandate has the interest of being one of the very few documents in Tytler's holograph to survive. In it he describes himself as 'James Tytler, Chemist at Restalrig', which may indicate where his most recent residence had been.

The state of the case now was that the two parties to a divorce action in Edinburgh were each represented by agents there while themselves separated by the widest possible distance: one virtually outside Scotland, in the obscurest corner of the Orkney Islands, and the other precisely so at the opposite extremity of the country. The oddity of the situation must have appealed to Elizabeth's solicitor Mr Anthony Woodhead, a jovial man with a reputation for eccentric humour, one of Burns's Edinburgh circle, to whom Tytler was probably known. His answers for the pursuer, dated 8 April (no doubt after another exchange of letters with Stromness), were couched in ironical terms, ridiculing the defence as 'of the dilatory kind'. Jean Aitkenhead's name, he pointed out, was not concealed from the defender, and as for the pursuer she was 'one of the daughters of the late James Rattray writer in Perth by Anne Blair his wife now also deceased. Her pedigree may be further traced if needfull.'

The next step to be taken was the usual formality of administering to the pursuer the oath *de calumnia*—that she had good reason to pursue her action and that there was no collusion between herself and the defender. To meet the obvious difficulty that Elizabeth was residing 'at Rackwick in Orkney' so that 'her coming to Edinburgh for the purpose of her deponing would be attended with very much trouble', Mr Woodhead presented a petition in her name on 23 April that her oath might be taken on commission. The commission was granted three days later in favour of William Young and Joshua Johnston, both writers in Stromness, and in due course the document returned to the Court with Elizabeth's oath recorded on the same sheet, dated 12 May. Her good firm signature to the oath is the only discoverable specimen of her writing.

At this point the action, though apparently simple enough, seems to run into difficulties. There is no further record of it, except that on 2 January 1789, eight months later, it went to *avizandum*, that is to say the judge announced that he would take time to consider his opinion. Presumably, then, Mr Woodhead representing Elizabeth had moved for judgment in December. The Commissary of Edinburgh who took the case to *avizandum* was Mr Robert Craig who had sat in the Commissary Court since 1773, a man of nearly sixty and of distinguished legal ancestry, on one side a Craig of Riccarton, on the other a Dundas of Arniston. It is hard to think that he found anything in the case to puzzle him—the marriage of the parties was on record and there could be no lack of witnesses to the defender's adulterous life; there is indeed a note that the case had been duly 'advised'. Presumably Elizabeth obtained her decree; but if so it was never 'extracted', which means that she took no steps to enforce it.

She could not do so effectually while Tytler remained in England, for no decree could be served on him there and he had no property in Edinburgh to arrest. This may explain her inaction and is perhaps evidence that Tytler did keep out of Scotland. Burns's statement written from Mauchline in November 1788 that Tytler 'drudges about Edinburgh' can, since Burns himself had not been there since March, mean nothing more certain than that Tytler formerly did so. In point of fact his wife's action against him marks the beginning of another hiatus in his traceable career. His exile may have been ended by either her dropping of her action against him or her death in Orkney. But of the latter there is no more positive evidence than of the former, since the parish registers of both Hoy and Stromness are missing over the relevant period. After the dating of Tytler's mandate from Berwick on 3 March 1788 there is no evidence of where he was or what he was doing for more than three years.

8

Seditious Libel

Tytler was back in Edinburgh at any rate by 1791 and possibly sooner. In that year he published a pamphlet and started yet another periodical.

The pamphlet was provoked by an article in the London *Critical Review* on a publication to which Tytler had been one of the contributors, *The Edinburgh Geographical, Commercial and Historical Grammar*. This had a rival in Guthrie's *Geographical, Historical, and Commercial Grammar*, an established work of which a revised edition had just come out. The *Critical Review* gave Guthrie the preference over the *Edinburgh Grammar* which had been published by Alexander Kincaid. Tytler therefore reviewed the reviewer, in a pamphlet which Kincaid published and which was 'sold by P. Hill and the other booksellers'. Meek considered it 'a most satirical and triumphant reply, which it was impossible to answer'. In it Tytler took particular exception to the *Critical Review*'s allegation that the Edinburgh publication merely plagiarized Guthrie. He gave a list of no less than 125 articles in it on subjects which he said were 'unnoticed in the twelfth or last edition of Guthrie', and on his final page he countered the *Review*'s statement that the *Edinburgh Grammar* had copied Guthrie's maps by listing 36 maps in it against only 21 in Guthrie. Moreover he affirmed that Guthrie's maps were all out of date anyway, having been reproduced from the work of Tytler's old acquaintance Thomas Salmon. He showed by many examples that the *Edinburgh Grammar* was more comprehensive and more up to date than Guthrie, and by many more that the latter was full of omissions, inaccuracies and inconsistencies. The editors of the *Critical Review* made no reply. It is of course possible that Tytler's scathing pamphlet never came to their notice.

The periodical, for Tytler's editorship of which Anderson is the authority, was entitled *The Historical Register*. It cost sixpence and appeared monthly from July 1791 to July 1792.

This was a year of rapidly rising political temperature which affected Tytler as it did thousands of others. Opinions on the course which the French Revolution was taking had become sharply divided in England, though less so in Scotland, since November 1790 when Burke published his *Reflections on the Revolution in France*, and many who had earlier watched it with sympathy were becoming uneasy. In February Thomas Paine replied to Burke in *The Rights of Man*, vindicating the principles of the French Revolution in vigorous and homely terms. Paine made no special reference to Scotland and his book at first had no great sale there; but it contributed indirectly to the agitation on political reform the demand for which had been stirring ever since the revolution in America.

In Scotland the franchise was restricted proportionately even more than in England, and from a combination of antique statutes and established tradition was enjoyed by an absurdly small minority. Scotland had only 45 representatives in the House of Commons, 30 returned by the counties, one by Edinburgh and the remaining 14 by the other 65 royal burghs in groups of four or five. The county voters never before the Reform Act of 1832 approached the number of 3000, even though their qualification to vote—holding land of a certain value from the Crown—was somewhat more widely spread by the creation of 'parchment barons' who held nominal superiorities but actually no property. The burgh voters were delegates from the town councils which were themselves almost private corporations. Moreover since only royal burghs might elect Members of Parliament, the small but numerous burghs of Fife absorbed two-fifths of all Scotland's burgh members, while growing and populous towns like Greenock and Falkirk had no representation at all.

The system with all its anomalies provided Scotland with M.P.s of generally respectable character and sometimes outstanding ability and conscientiousness; but none achieved a position of real influence except the brilliant Henry Dundas, the devoted ally of William Pitt. In the General Election of 1790 he became M.P. for Edinburgh, Sir Adam Fergusson returning to his former seat for Ayrshire; and in 1791 he became Secretary of State for the Northern Department.

That the system worked reasonably well was no defence against its many critics. As a representative system it was in fact indefensible and attempts at reforming the franchise, none of them however very radical, had been made more than once. Now the movement for reform was spreading, with especial urgency in the burghs, in most of which administration was inefficient, sluggish and often corrupt. New social conditions, arising from the progress of trade and industry, were creating independent thought among the middle and lower classes.

To these stirrings the popular upheaval in France gave a new stimulus. The movement for reform was promoted by men of position and high character such as Lord Gardenstone, a Lord of Session, Henry Erskine, who had been briefly Lord Advocate, John Clerk of Eldin and Archibald Fletcher; but after the revolution in France had begun it became the cover for every kind of agitator, from the serious to the crank, from the public-spirited to the merely mischievous. The cause of reform suffered inevitable damage. Pitt's moderate inclination towards it faded away, and Dundas, whose power in manipulating Scottish elections depended on the limitation of the franchise, turned from indifference to firm opposition. There was also and not unnaturally a growing dread of Jacobinism. As events in France moved steadily downwards towards extremism and anarchy, there came to birth among the 'friends of administration' in Great Britain an identification of reform with revolution which in the event set back the cause of reform for another generation.

It was in this atmosphere of fermenting aspirations, as urgent as they were vague, that Tytler launched the last of his Scottish periodicals, the *Historical Register*, of which the first number appeared on 1 July 1791. As might have been expected, his warm heart and shallow intellect responded to popular feeling in its most romantic, even melodramatic form. The tone of the *Historical Register* was considerably more heated and advanced than the views of moderate reformers, and it made no secret of sympathy with the French Revolution, asserting in its issue of October 1791 that 'the example of some other states of Europe who had so nobly and so successfully asserted the rights of man could not fail to awaken the attention of Scotsmen to their true interest, after which it was impossible that they could long continue in a state of wretched slavery'.

The opening months of 1792 gave the Government cause for increasing uneasiness. In February Paine published a sequel or second part to *The Rights of Man*, comparing the British Constitution disadvantageously to those of the United States and France and also making a number of proposals for new or better social services. The latter, including such measures as old age pensions and maternity and funeral grants, are the commonplaces of the modern welfare state but in their time were revolutionary and calculated—or so the Government might reasonably consider—to arouse general discontent. In April the French forced their captive King to declare war on Austria, making it clear that the effects of the Revolution could not be regarded as to be confined within the borders of France; and in the same month there was founded in England the Society of the Friends of the People.

The coincidence was unfortunate, for the Friends of the People began as a body standing only for political reform, not for revolution, and openly professing its opposition to the more radical associations which had recently sprung up in England to propagate the teachings of Paine. It had no branches; its subscription was too high to interest people of the lower classes in joining it; and its leaders, who included Sheridan and Charles Grey (the future Prime Minister

Earl Grey), were by no means extremists even though they also included the hot-headed Earl of Lauderdale whose early enthusiasm for the French Revolution had earned him the nickname of 'Citizen Maitland'.

Bodies of a very different complexion attracted much larger membership, and the Government took alarm. After all, it was in political clubs and by insidious pamphleteers that the French Revolution had been carefully prepared and fostered, and their imitators were now appearing in Great Britain in ominous numbers. The very word reform took on sinister implications. The measure for Scottish burgh reform which Sheridan brought forward and pressed in a rather tactless speech was emphatically defeated in the Commons on 18 April.

Dundas was perturbed by what a friend of his described as 'an almost universal spirit of reform and opposition to the established government and legal administration which has wonderfully diffused through the manufacturing towns of this country and is openly patronized by many gentlemen of fortune'. He persuaded Pitt to issue on 21 May a proclamation against 'seditious writings' which he had himself drafted a fortnight earlier. It aroused strong feelings. On the one hand the 'friends of administration' poured in loyal addresses in support of it. On the other the reformers abused it as repressive and tyrannical. In the Commons Dundas had defended it as made necessary by the wide circulation of Thomas Paine's writings and the formation of clubs and societies to carry out his ideas.

Tytler attacked the proclamation in the *Historical Register*, affirming that its effect would be to make magistrates accusers instead of judges—a criticism which he had taken up from a London paper, the *Morning Chronicle*. But one result of it in Scotland was the very opposite of what had been intended. It stimulated a demand for copies of Paine's *Rights of Man*. Of all 'seditious writings' it was the most notorious but in Scotland it had hitherto sold very sluggishly. According to a report in July, people in all parts of Scotland now eagerly inquired for 'the book that is forbidden to be sold', and an Edinburgh book-seller who had found his stock of *The Rights of Man* almost unsaleable, sold it all off and supplied repeat orders, at an enhanced price. Not for the first or last time, official disapproval had defeated its own ends and censorship turned out the most effective publicity.

Political unrest increased, and Henry Dundas, not without justice, was generally blamed among reformers for the rejection of Sheridan's motion for burgh reform. He received anonymous letters of abuse and later in the year threats of assassination, neither of which perturbed him in the least. It was Dundas who had spoken in the Commons of the grievances of Scottish burgesses as 'supposed and unsubstantiated' and his nephew and son-in-law Robert Dundas, the Lord Advocate, who had alleged that if such grievances existed the Court of Session had all the necessary powers to redress them. There was a strong anti-Dundas flavour in the riots which took place in Edinburgh early in June.

These disorders began with the traditional revels attending the annual observance of the King's Birthday on the 4th. This festival was regularly celebrated by the drinking of the royal health by the magistrates and a large party of official guests. The meeting was held in the Parliament House with such jollity of 'roaring, drinking, toasting, and quarrelling' as, according to Lord Cockburn's recollections, 'made the Court stink for a week with the wreck and the fumes'. The Edinburgh mob imitated their betters with even rowdier enthusiasm, and generally took the occasion to harass their traditional enemy the City Guard.

This year the civic authorities awaited the anniversary with some nervousness. The ferment accompanying the reform movement might add viciousness to the usual disorder and there were rumours that the customary riot would be something special. 'The Scotch are bad mobbers', wrote Cockburn nearly 40 years later. 'They are too serious at it; they never joke; and they throw stones.' The Lord Provost took precautions. He was given the disposal of a regiment of foot and four troops of dragoons. But this display of force when the day arrived roused rather than cowed the spirit of the mob. They threw squibs and crackers among the horses, stoned the soldiers, some of whom were severely hurt, and tore down the City Guard's sentry-box and made a bonfire of it. The troops cleared the streets before midnight but it was half-past two in the morning before it was felt safe to withdraw the last detachment.

Next day a meeting of respectable citizens was held in the High Kirk and soothingly addressed by the Lord Advocate, Robert Dundas. He was a pleasant little man of no particular talent and a notoriously poor speaker. His efforts to allay public alarm were stultified by ensuing events. That evening a small crowd gathered in George Square, at that time the most fashionable quarter of Edinburgh, where he lived and also, near by, his aunt, Henry Dundas's mother, known in the old Scots fashion as Lady Arniston, an old lady of 86 of remarkable character and intellectual vigour. It was before her house that the people gathered with jeers and huzzas, parading with mockery an effigy of Mr Secretary Dundas. Lady Arniston, contemptuous of the rabble, remained perfectly calm, and the Sheriff of Edinburgh, John Pringle, arriving with a guard of soldiers and repeating the short formula of the Riot Act from memory, succeeded in dispersing them. But an hour later they re-assembled in George Square in larger numbers, 'as thick as they could stand', and now in much more dangerous mood. A crash of glass was followed by the cry 'There goes the Lord Advocate's windows!' Once more the troops were summoned. This time they fired on the mob, who suffered five or six casualties and quickly melted away.

The following evening the mob reappeared in George Square but finding soldiers already posted there they did not risk another clash with them. They slipped away to St Andrew Square in the New Town and there broke the windows of the Lord Provost.

Although a reward of 100 guineas was offered for the detection of the ringleaders of these tumults no one was found responsible and it is probable that they were quite spontaneous. They did however give some colour to the Government's coupling together of reform and riot, and the recollection of them formed a sinister background to the first meeting in Scotland of a Society of the Friends of the People which was held in Edinburgh on 26 July. In the autumn branches were founded in Glasgow, Dundee, Perth and other places. The difference between them and the English prototype was that members were welcomed for a low subscription, and their ranks were swelled by small shopkeepers and craftsmen.

The rapid increase of the Friends of the People caused Dundas, who visited Edinburgh in October and November, much concern. The Friends were avowedly constitutionalists and opposed to all sedition and disorder. But they were joined by not a few with much wider grievances, in whom emotion ruled rather than reason and who were impatient of any prudence or restraint. Among these recruits, according to Chambers, was James Tytler, who, as Anderson recalled, 'associated with discontented persons', a vague but suggestive phrase.

The events of this year increased his ardour for reform, and he saw the need for it on every side, not merely in the state of the franchise. About this time he published a pamphlet on the excise, 'a deliberate exposition', says Anderson, 'of the abuses of government', and he did not refrain from personal invective, attacking various excise officials, one in particular, by name, or at least by identifiable initials.

Tytler attacked individual targets in the *Historical Register* as well. The motto he had chosen for the magazine was 'Nothing extenuate', and his omission of '—nor set down aught in malice' might well have been deliberate. In its pages he accused the Lord Advocate of having, in his speech in the High Kirk on 5 June, 'artfully insinuated that there was a premeditated design of the people of Edinburgh to rise in revolt'. These personal attacks were imprudent. To assail authors with whom he disagreed or critics whose strictures he resented was one thing but to bring charges against public officials quite another. He was again achieving notoriety but it was of a dangerous kind.

On the appearance of its tenth number the *Historical Register* began to be issued in two parts or rather in two editions. One bore the sub-title *The Edinburgh Monthly Intelligencer* and continued the paper's original policy of advocating reform. The other was sub-titled *The Universal Monthly Intelligencer* and was much more violent, combining propaganda for reform with attacks on abuses of every kind, many of which had nothing to do with administration, such as the extravagance of the Court and the rapacity of Highland landlords. It also castigated the slave trade, to which Tytler, according to Meek, was warmly opposed. To reformers it held up French examples for imitation. Above all, it urged, they should combine to form an unanimous front, until their numbers were enough for them to form something like the National Convention which had just been established in France, and of which Paine, who had prudently slipped out of England, had been elected a member.

In August, just after publishing this inflammatory suggestion, Tytler brought the *Historical Register* to an end. He had secured work which promised to be more remunerative than the conduct of a periodical and moreover very much to his taste and capacity. An Edinburgh surgeon had invited him to compile a system of surgery in three volumes, 'ghosting' a work to which the surgeon was to put his name. Tytler was busily engaged on this book in the autumn of 1792. But his enthusiasm for reform was unabated and during November he contributed to its cause a publication which, though quite short and perhaps even only casually thrown off, had more effect on his fortunes than anything else he ever wrote. It led indeed to his ruin and exile.

November brought events both abroad and at home to increase the Government's anxiety. On the 16th the French National Convention issued a decree that the navigation of the Scheldt should be free to all nations, a direct defiance to Great Britain which had only four

years before guaranteed the independence of the Dutch Nether-
lands. On the 19th the Convention gave further evidence of its intention to meddle with the affairs of other nations. It was warmly
receiving addresses of sympathy from the radical societies in England, and it now made a declaration of international fraternity,
promising French help to all peoples who were striving for liberty.
This could only be regarded, in Great Britain as elsewhere, as
deliberately hostile to established governments. 'Nothing but our
being ready for war can preserve peace', wrote Pitt to Dundas.
Plans were made to call out part of the English militia, a step which
was generally approved. 'Every wise man', wrote Lord Fife, who
might rank as one himself, on 14 December, 'will think Government
rather delayed too long in putting the country in a state of defence', adding in unconscious echo of Pitt, 'The best and most
prudent way to avoid war is to be prepared for it.'

In Scotland there was at this time no militia, successive adminis-
trations ever since the last Jacobite rising having remained stub-
bornly convinced that Scotsmen could not be trusted except in the
regular army with arms in their hands. It had long been a national
complaint, recalled only a few years before this by Burns among
Scotland's grievances against the House of Commons—'Her *lost
Militia* fir'd her bluid.' But pressure of events was now about to
remove it, for it was clear that a more widely disposed force than
the regular troops was needed to ensure both the defence of the
realm and the preservation of order. 'As we have no militia, you
should give us Lord Lieutenants and [a] fencible force', Dundas was
told by Lord Adam Gordon, the Commander-in-Chief in Scotland.
Dundas agreed and acted without delay. At the beginning of
January 1793 he introduced into the Commons a Scots Militia Bill
which, as the *Caledonian Mercury* commented, was 'expected to meet
with little or no opposition, although all former attempts have
proved ineffectual'. Then at last a Lord Lieutenant was appointed
for each county of Scotland with the authority (which continued
till 1882) to raise a militia regiment and appoint its officers.

Meanwhile in 1792 though there were some troops stationed in Scotland they were few in number and concentrated in the customary garrisons. They were not available to prevent some ominous rioting in several towns during November. There was disorder at the docks in Leith and Aberdeen, where the sailors went on strike and unrigged ships preparing for sea. In Dundee a formidable mob paraded the streets shouting 'Liberty and equality!' They broke windows, lit a large bonfire in the High Street, and set up and decorated a Tree of Liberty, a form of demonstration imported from France, the symbol of revolution. Another such Tree was planted in Perth where however the rioters were less violent. There and elsewhere Dundas was burnt in effigy.

The Friends of the People strove hard but in vain to dissociate themselves from all such manifestations. Their Dundee society on 21 November unanimously adopted resolutions to the effect 'that every member of this Society shall express his abhorrence of riots and disorderly meetings, and promise to do every thing in his power to prevent them'. The Government however continued to regard the Friends of the People with suspicion, and determined but moderate reformers, men like Henry Erskine and Archibald Fletcher, refused to join them. Yet their leaders were men who could hardly be thought likely revolutionaries—the Earl of Selkirk's son Lord Daer, Colonel William Dalrymple of Fordel, Colonel Norman Macleod, M.P. for Inverness-shire, and a group of advocates who included Thomas Muir of Huntershill. They were all however marked men already. Dalrymple, Macleod, and Lord Sempill, a Scottish peer who favoured reform, were deprived of their commissions in the Army.

The Lord Advocate had one or two active and intelligent informers who attended meetings of the Edinburgh Society of the Friends of the People. From their information the Sheriff, John Pringle, wrote on 24 November a report to Henry Dundas which described one such meeting. 'Last night', it says, 'there was a private meeting of the Delegates from the different Societies of the

Friends of the People in the house of Mr Buchanan, baker in the Canongate, for the purpose of receiving the resolutions that had been adopted at the previous meeting. The resolutions then exhibited were 1st a compleat and general reform of the burrows [*sic*], 2dly a reform of the excise laws. Col. Macleod, Col. Dalrymple, Mr Millar and Mr Muir, advocates, and some others gave it as their opinion that this should be effectuated by an application to Parliament. Others said that they had nothing to do with Parliament if they had the majority of the People with them. . . . I understand the majority of the meeting were in favor of the more moderate opinion.'

Tytler is unlikely to have been the delegate of one of the Societies and there is no reason to think that he was himself present at this meeting, but he must have received an account of it from someone who was there and who was probably not one of the moderate majority. Tytler himself certainly did not share the majority's opinion and he at once took fire. Within the next two days he composed and had printed a broadside, addressed 'To the People and their Friends', which expressed with the utmost violence the view which they had outvoted.

'Mr Tytler's zeal to propagate his opinions,' says Meek, 'was exceedingly ill timed and dangerous to himself.' It was in fact this broadside that led directly to his prosecution.

No copy of it seems to have survived—Meek, though he had formerly seen one, was unable to find one in 1805—but its text was given in full in Tytler's indictment and is here reproduced (see Appendix). It is a wild attack on Parliament, with every appearance of having been written in tremendous haste. Tytler adjured those who desired reform not to trust their leaders who advised them to petition Parliament—'certain Colonels and Captains', an obvious allusion to Dalrymple and Macleod. Parliament, he declared, was itself unworthy of trust. 'You must consider the House of Commons as your enemies. They affect to consider themselves as the *democratical* part of the constitution. They are not; they are a vile junto

124

of aristocrats. The majority of them are landholders; and every landholder is a despot, in the most true and literal sense of the word'—a condemnation hardly tactful since it would include Dalrymple, Macleod and even Muir, with many other Friends of the People besides. Tytler advised his readers, if they wanted results, to petition not Parliament but the King, and to ask him to dissolve Parliament and allow the people to elect representatives 'of good understanding and character' but not 'landholders'. He added the injunction, 'Let not the minister, or his *spies*, however, deceive you by promising a reform, and admitting the inferior class of landholders as electors, or capable of being elected, as I am told he has offered. Thus you would be overwhelmed with an inundation of tyrants . . . and instead of obtaining any reform, the chains of the nation will be rivetted.'

Tytler was stated in his indictment to have employed a printer named William Turnbull to print 500 copies of this effusion, to have received them on 26 November—within three days of the meeting in the baker's house in the Canongate—and to have distributed some 250 of them in 'the city of Edinburgh and its suburbs'. A few days later, it was affirmed, he added another paragraph, got Turnbull to print it on the back of the remaining copies and circulated them also. This afterthought was even stronger meat than the main text. It declared that if the King would not hear the suggested petition the unrepresented people need pay no taxes, for that was laid down in Magna Charta. 'The conclusion is, if the King hear you not, keep your money in your pockets, and frame your own laws, and the minority must submit to the majority.'

With his usual bad luck Tytler published this broadside at the very moment when it was most likely to get him into trouble. On 1 December Dundas addressed a circular letter to the Sheriffs in the various Scottish counties where disorders had occurred requiring them in the strictest terms to take note of the proclamation against seditious writings of 21 May. They were ordered 'to make diligent enquiry respecting all such wicked and seditious writings' and to report the results to the Lord Advocate. From Edinburgh Sheriff Pringle replied on 7 December, 'I shall use my utmost endeavour to discharge this important part of my duty'. He was as good as his word. Only two days later he laid hands on the printers of a pamphlet called *The Political Progress of Britain, or an Impartial Account of the Principal Abuses in the Government of the Country from the Revolution in 1688*. And he had already apprehended James Tytler.

As December drew on and news came from France that Louis XVI had been placed on trial by his own subjects, the rumblings of agitation in Scotland seemed to the authorities more and more ominous. The Lord Advocate received reports not only of discussions at political meetings but of strange rumours spreading among the rural workers that 'liberty and equality' meant a dividing up of all landed property so that they would all be 'equally free and equally rich'; of industrial workers being 'poisoned with an enthusiastic rage for ideal liberty'; and of such toasts in Edinburgh taverns as 'George III and last and damnation to all crowned heads!'—even though many such sentiments were uttered in what the informer himself called 'the unguarded effervescence of conviviality'.

There were also a few reports of attempts to tamper with the loyalty of soldiers stationed in Edinburgh which, however, met with no success at all. One such attempt was inquired into with great thoroughness. It had taken place in front of the new Register House. Though not completed at the back till more than 30 years later, this stately building had at last been sufficiently finished for all the scattered public records in Edinburgh to be collected into it and for the Lord Clerk Register's small staff to open it for business in 1789. The Register House was regarded with pride as the first public building in the New Town and moreover the first in the United Kingdom specifically designed and erected to hold public records; sentries were regularly posted there for whom a small

126

guard-house (long ago demolished) had been included in Adam's plans.

Early in November one of the sentries on duty at the Register House, a certain Nehemiah Perrins of the 37th regiment, was approached in the night-time by two strangers who engaged him in conversation. One of the Lord Advocate's spies, lingering as near as he dared, overheard the suspicious words 'liberty and equality'. The two men got no change out of Private Perrins, who when questioned later confirmed that they had been suggesting that he and his comrades should desert. One of them he described as having been 'dressed in a drab coloured coat and white stockings' and 'about five foot six inches in height'—but the sergeant of the guard who had also observed the incident put his stature at an inch taller. Five foot seven was just Tytler's measurement, but the coincidence is not enough to incriminate him. Later a man was arrested and identified by Perrins and the sergeant. His name proved to be John Molle. 'His brother who is a Writer to the Signet came and bail'd him out', Perrins's lieutenant-colonel reported to Lord Adam Gordon, 'and says he can prove an *alibi* and that there is a person in Edinburgh so like his brother that he is often mistaken for him.'

This and other occurrences were more than enough to stir the Lord Advocate to action. He was a kindly and likeable man and moderate in his opinions. But he was under pressure from his inflexible uncle and the rest of the Government, and moreover he could not be unaffected by the agitation and fears of his ordinary acquaintances, not merely the determined 'friends of administration' but unbiassed and fair-minded people whom the terrible news from France and the rumours of sinister plottings in their own country filled with profound and not unreasonable alarm. He was certainly not of the stuff of which tyrants and oppressors are made. But he had and could not delegate to anyone the responsibility for legal action against incendiaries, and he could not but regard the more extreme members of the societies of the Friends of the People as coming under that description.

He took care therefore to have one of his agents present at the first conference of delegates from all the Scottish societies of Friends of the People which took place in Edinburgh on 11, 12 and 13 December. It was held in a dancing-school in James's Court on the north side of the Lawnmarket. The moderates were again distinctly in the majority—several delegates were ministers of the Church—and the resolutions passed reflected their and not the extremists' views; but the gathering seriously impressed the Lord Advocate by its evidence of the strength of the reform movement. His agent was able to report a great many of the delegates' names. They came from no less than 80 societies of Friends of the People in different parts of central Scotland.

It was at this conference that Thomas Muir drew attention to himself by his insistent demand that it should welcome and reply to a communication dated 23 November from the Society of United Irishmen which Wolfe Tone had organized in 1791. But the meeting, feeling that some phrases in the letter had a treasonable flavour about them, firmly rejected the proposal. Muir's behaviour during this incident confirmed the judgment of Archibald Fletcher whom he had vainly pressed to join the Friends of the People and who considered him 'an honest enthusiast, but . . . an ill-judging man.'

On 13 December Robert Dundas was able to send his uncle a very complete report from his agent—'the minutes of the proceedings of the delegates from the Societies. We are endeavouring', he went on, 'to get hold of the letter which is alluded to as treasonable; and it may probably be furnished me this evening. In that event, the Solicitor [Robert Blair] and I are resolved to lay Muir by the heels on a charge of High Treason. You need not be reminded of the necessity of keeping the information we now regularly receive, secret. . . . I really think every thing *now* goes on in this country as well as you can possibly wish. Dalrymple is frightened out of his wits. . . .'

On 16 December Pringle told Henry Dundas that he had not yet managed to get a copy of 'the paper from Ireland, of which so much

6 John Bull dancing to the music of Pitt and Dundas

mention is made in the debate' but the very next day he was able to send one. Preparations now went forward for the series of trials for treason which opened the following month. There were not a great many of them—22 in all within the next 30 years—and they served their purpose of damping down what revolutionary spirit there might have been. But the early ones have become notorious, attracting the interest and indignation of countless historians on account of the judges' extreme strictness in interpreting the law against sedition, amounting to actual bias against the panels. Thomas Muir's sentence of transportation has in particular earned him a sort of canonization to which he was scarcely entitled. Yet little sympathy has been shown for the first man selected for an example as a seditious agitator though he never actually appeared before the Court of Justiciary—the much less romantic figure of James Tytler.

Tytler had probably come under official observation in the recent months for his aggressive articles in the *Historical Register* and for his libellous pamphlet on the excise. What else, until he published his broadside *To the People and their Friends*, brought him under suspicion is uncertain. There is very little likelihood that he was the man in the drab coat and white stockings who seemed to be Mr Molle's double. Yet his immediate arrest, probably on the very day when Dundas's admonitory circular to the Sheriff reached Edinburgh, suggests that Pringle had had his eye on him before he began his inquiries after 'seditious writings'. Tytler was at any rate at once indicted for publishing 'a seditious libel' which he had 'circulated among the inhabitants of a populous city, the metropolis of a country'. A publication which urged its readers to defy Parliament and withhold payment of their taxes was undoubtedly subversive, but it is hard to see why it should have been picked out for the very first prosecution. Tytler was, it is true, a fairly familiar figure in Edinburgh but nobody could have thought of him as an influential one.

Perhaps the explanation is simply that he happened to be the first seditious writer arrested, and that someone had brought him and his frothy little broadside directly to the Lord Advocate's notice immediately it appeared. It is quite possible that people ready to do him a bad turn were not wanting. Tytler wielded at times a poisonous pen, easily provoked, and more than one author or printer whose product he had abused, or petty official whose conduct he had attacked, may have been waiting for a chance of revenge. All that was necessary was for someone to hand a copy of *To the People and their Friends* to the Lord Advocate.

One possible informer at least can be suggested. Among the 20 witnesses cited to appear against Tytler in the High Court, who included Turnbull the printer of the broadside and two of his assistants, were another printer, Charles Stewart, and also John Caw, warehouseman to Messrs Stewart, Ruthven & Co., printers in Edinburgh. Charles Stewart, who later became printer to the University of Edinburgh, was one of the founders and publishers of the *Edinburgh Herald*, a recently established newspaper first published on 15 March 1790. It was the one Edinburgh periodical which stood uncompromisingly against reform. The highly respected man of letters Henry Mackenzie described it to Robert Dundas as 'the only newspaper in Scotland *truly* and *sincerely* affected to Government', and the Lord Advocate was so much in agreement as to subsidize it with a payment of £400 which he advanced on his own responsibility and wrote three times to his uncle asking for repayment of the sum as money well spent. Whether Charles Stewart had a personal grudge against Tytler or not, he must have regarded his politics with horror and probably Tytler himself as a dangerous person who ought in the public interest to be silenced.

Tytler was arrested on 4 December, that is to say as soon as the Sheriff received Dundas's circular requiring action against seditious writings. He was at this time living, according to Chambers, in 'the house of a friend in a solitary situation on the northern skirts of Salisbury Crags', a statement confirmed by the indictment which described him as 'James Tytler, chemist, residing in King's Park, in the neighbourhood of Edinburgh'. From that airy situation Tytler could survey his old refuge the Sanctuary of Holyrood, which could be no asylum to him now.

He was taken before the Sheriff and signed some sort of declaration on which he was released but cited to appear before the Court of Justiciary on 7 January 1793. Two of the Edinburgh booksellers to whom he was so well known signed a bond of caution for his appearance under penalty of 600 merks Scots, a modest sum equivalent to only £33 6s 8d sterling.

There is ample evidence that the juries for the treason trials were as far as possible packed to secure convictions, though the packing did not make conviction quite such a certainty as is generally assumed. 'I hope, not without some anxiety', wrote Robert Dundas to his uncle on 3 January, 'that an Edinburgh jury will do equal justice on our seditious gentry that a Middlesex one has done with you. Three trials of this kind come on this ensuing week.' Next day he wrote, 'Our trials commence on Monday, and we have three ready for next week. . . . We have taken up two nights ago Muir the lawyer. . . . He has been discovered circulating in the West Country Paine's works &c and particularly the pamphlet herein inclosed, which appears to be more within the reach of the law than anything I have yet met with.' He expressed his hope that the latter would enable him 'to bring this ringleader of sedition immediately before a jury'.

The day for which Tytler had been cited arrived, 7 January 1793. But Tytler had vanished. The proceedings which drove him from his native land were therefore brief. His name was called in the High Court and he did not appear. It was called three times more at the door of the Court and still he did not appear. The Lord Advocate then moved for sentence of fugitation and outlawry and the forfeit of Tytler's bail.

In the form used for centuries past, sentence was given. James

Tytler was 'to be put to His Highnesses horn, and all his moveable goods and gear to be escheat and inbrought to His Majesty's use for his contempt and disobedience in not appearing this day and place.' The bond of caution granted by James Hunter and Robert Ross, booksellers in Edinburgh, under penalty of 600 merks Scots was to be forfeited.

That evening the *Caledonian Mercury* reported in a brief paragraph the trial and outlawry of 'the well-known James Tytler, chemist', and the Lord Advocate wrote to his uncle:

My dear Sir;
I enclose you the indictment against Tytler, on which he has been this day fugitated for non-appearance. I leave to your own consideration the propriety of advertizing a reward for his apprehension.
Yours ever
R. DUNDAS.
An extract of the sentence of fugitation shall be sent by this post.

On 9 January the Lord Advocate wrote, 'I really think it material that Tytler if in London should be apprehended', and a few days later he was coupling him with another delinquent who had also slipped his bail and disappeared, William Stewart, merchant in Leith, 'a smart-looking young man, about 23 years of age', accused along with one John Elder of publishing a pamphlet called *The Rights of Man Delineated, and the Origin of Government*. Steward was outlawed for non-appearance on 10 January and on the 13th the Lord Advocate wrote to Henry Dundas as follows:

'Tytler is, I am informed, gone to Ireland. I have no information as to Stewart. In the Caledonian Mercury [for 12 January] you will observe a reward of Fifty Guineas offered for his apprehension. I am indifferent whether they are apprehended or not. But it would have the most beneficial effects on the minds of people here if they saw both these persons advertized in the London and Dublin Gazette; as it would prove to them the determination of Government to proceed to the utmost extremity—the Dublin Gazette particularly.'

According to Meek, Tytler 'had declared he would disdain to shrink back from a fair trial, if he had any prospect of an upright jury: but being extremely doubtful as to this particular, he resolved to abscond'. This statement, written twelve years later, was probably coloured by recollection of the notorious trials of Muir, Palmer, Gerrard and others. Tytler had no precedent from which to form so pessimistic a forecast. Even if convicted he would almost certainly, like the other small fry, have got off with a light sentence of imprisonment. It is likely that he merely panicked.

9

The Land of the Free

Tytler remained in Ireland for over two years. If the authorities did make any attempt to apprehend him it cannot have been very earnest. Probably they did not, after a month or two, think him worth pursuing. Of how he managed to live, in a country where he had no friends and no connections, there is no evidence. He continued, however, to write.

Jean and her twin daughters had been left in Edinburgh without any means of support. Paterson says that 'they were never able to rejoin him', but this, as will appear, is not true. They were for the moment none the less, in Meek's words, 'wholly destitute of the means of subsistence', and in her distress Jean applied for help to Colin Macfarquhar, one of those who had profited so handsomely from Tytler's years of toil on the *Encyclopaedia Britannica*. Macfarquhar treated her with brutal callousness. He listened to her story and then 'peremptorily ordered her down stairs', saying, with reference to Tytler's attack on the exciseman, 'that her husband had written against a much better man than himself'.

Nevertheless the family survived, and by some means or other joined Tytler in Ireland, probably in Belfast.

Tytler completed the system of surgery which he had been ghosting, and according to Meek it 'made its appearance in three volumes octavo'. I have not been able to trace this work, for which it seems, from Meek's rather confused account of it, that Tytler failed to secure his promised payment. It may be the same as what Anderson mentions as a system not of surgery but of chemistry, which he notes as 'written at the expence of a gentleman who was to put his name to it, unpublished'.

Tytler also produced at least two pamphlets during his time in Ireland. One, said to have been published in Belfast in 1794, was in reply to a new work of Paine's, *The Age of Reason*, a crude and violent defence of Deism or 'natural religion' against Christianity which had appeared in 1793 and increased the odium in which Paine was held. Possibly Tytler hoped that by turning from politics to theology and controverting the scandalous Paine he might begin to rehabilitate himself in the eyes of the orthodox.

The other pamphlet may be the same as what Anderson mentions under the title of *Remarks on Mr Pinkerton's Introduction to the History of Scotland*. John Pinkerton was an antiquary and historian of no mean ability who did some valuable research and accurately published many old Scottish poems and historical documents. But he was a crotchety and aggressive person, with a remarkable capacity for annoying people who had encouraged him, and extremely opinionated. One of his quirks, first asserted in print in 1787, was that the Celts had no distinctive racial entity and were merely a branch of the Goths. Tytler went for him in a pamphlet of 40 pages entitled *A Dissertation on the Origin and Antiquity of the Scottish Nation*. 'Mr Pinkerton', he wrote, 'seems to have outdone all his predecessors in zeal against the antiquity of Scotland, and has delivered himself in terms so pedantic, insolent and opprobrious, as certainly deserve the severest reprehension. . . . Our author has found means to fill Britain and Scotland with a kind of mongrel nation, which may occasionally be either Welsh, Scythian, Goths, Irish, or Scots, as he pleases.'

The pamphlet was published with Tytler's name on the title-page, in London, and described as 'printed for the booksellers'. This seems to imply that 'the booksellers' had got hold of a manuscript of Tytler's and published it without his authority for their own profit; but there cannot have been much profit in such a work and the probability is that Tytler had sold them the copyright for what it would fetch. The *Dissertation* appeared in 1795 and in the early part of that year he had an urgent motive to raise money. For he had decided to emigrate with his family to the United States of America.

It was about midsummer when they sailed from Belfast in the brig *Eliza*, Captain William Fairfield, bound for Salem in Massachusetts. The *Eliza* carried 10 cabin passengers and 65 in the steerage, and it may be safely presumed that the Tytler family were among the latter and endured all the hardship, confinement and tedium that an Atlantic crossing in a small ship could entail. But Tytler, accustomed as he was to hard lying and frugal comforts, could disregard them. He felt himself to be a martyr in the cause of liberty, and his habitual benevolence towards the whole human race except those who annoyed him was undiminished by his prosecution. He was bound for the land of the free, and he looked forward eagerly to breathing the larger air of a country which knew no King or Lord Advocate, which allowed every citizen a voice in electing the legislative body, with a chance to use it every second year, and where treason consisted only in levying war against the state or adhering to its enemies. He blew off some of his enthusiasm and whiled away a part of the voyage by composing a poem—which when published ran to 24 pages of print—entitled *The Rising of the Sun in the West, or the Origin and Progress of Liberty.*

The *Eliza*'s passengers were, it seems, all emigrants intending to settle in America. Most of them were 'mechanics'; some were men of education, and a few bore names—Dalrymple, Dunlap and Lemon—which were later to become respected in the history of Salem. The Dunlap family were joining a son already settled there. People crowded together for several weeks in a brig could not fail to become acquainted, and Tytler gained friendly notice from some of his fellow-passengers, which was of service to him later on.

They reached Salem on 8 August 1795. It was a flourishing town of some 9,000 people on the irregularly indented coast of Massachusetts some 20 miles north of Boston, with a history going back to 1626. Its harbour faced south and it had numerous other quays, coves and anchorages provided by the neighbouring inlets of the sea. Ships were built here and all the auxiliary industries were well established, rope walks, cooperages and tanneries. Salem was the principal town of Essex County and was a centre of business and commerce. There was a considerable coastwise and overseas trade, and its prosperity was reflected in the large and handsome houses built by the successful merchants of Salem. In one of these on Essex Street lived a Unitarian minister, Mr William Bentley, whose diary throws much light on Salem life of those days and has several allusions to Tytler.

The farms and orchards of Essex County did not attract Tytler to return to the country life of his boyhood. For most of his life he had been a townsman and it was in Salem that he settled. Here were the industry and enterprise which might give scope to his various talents; here were two newspapers, the *Gazette* and the *Register*, to which he might contribute; and here were printers to give him occasional or even permanent commissions. Though Salem was much smaller than Edinburgh, only a provincial town, and its climate much more extreme in both winter and summer, it was a place in which he might hope to rebuild his life and even at the age of 50, when by the standards of those days he was becoming an old man, to begin a new career. No one knew more of his background than he chose to tell them. He was accepted as 'a well known chemist, forced to leave his native country on account of his political views'; he was an author with work on the *Encyclopaedia Britannica* to his credit; no one doubted that he was married to Jean Aitkenhead, whom he described as his third wife—as by this time she may have been, whether bigamously or not. In the new country where he was settling he could expect sympathy untainted by prejudice.

The Dunlaps spoke of him to Mr Bentley when the latter dined with them within a week of their landing, and showed him *The Rising of the Sun in the West*. Mr Bentley did not think much of its

137

flatulent rhetoric. 'It might have been a rhapsody adapted to the character of the time', he observed, if it had been published at the beginning of the Revolution 20 years earlier. It was printed, but it had no great sale, even though its title-page claimed the goodwill of American readers for 'one of the compilers of the Encyclopedia Brittanica [*sic*] in Scotland, exiled from that country on account of his writings in the cause of liberty'.

Having little money and no resources but his brains, Tytler had some difficulty in finding a home. He at length settled on the rocky peninsula known as Salem Neck which jutted north-eastwards from the east end of the town. The Neck, little more than 100 acres in extent, was as yet sparsely inhabited. It contained two or three small farms and there were fortifications on the headlands which at this time did not need to be garrisoned. It was 'in the barracks of the new fort on the height of land', presumably unoccupied, that Tytler and his family found accommodation, and this probably indicates Fort Juniper at the extreme end of the Neck. It was a place remote but not distant from Salem: a few minutes' walk would bring Tytler to the Neck Gate, the narrow spit of land which joined the Neck to the mainland and led into Derby Street. The spot had moreover the advantage of being close to some clam banks from which Tytler and his wife could add to their scanty provisions. They were the best banks that he had ever heard of, he remarked: 'they discount daily, and cannot fail'.

He set to earning his living by the same miscellaneous means as in Edinburgh, preparing medicines for apothecaries, writing for the *Gazette*, and continuing to experiment in chemistry. In 1796 he wrote another counterblast to Thomas Paine—*Paine's Second Part of the Age of Reason answered*—which was published in July in an edition of 300 copies at 25 cents each; and about the same time he embarked on the last of his scientific and commercial projects. Once more he conceived an idea which seemed progressive and promising, failed in execution, but might well have prospered in the hands of anyone less consistently unlucky than Tytler. The scheme was simple, indeed obvious. Here he was settled on the shore of the Atlantic, close to a prosperous and growing seaport where ships had to be provisioned for long voyages. What could seem a more useful and profitable enterprise than the establishment of some salt pans?

He set to work in Watch House Cove, probably along the beach between Fort Juniper and Watch House Point, 'rolling rocks' with his own hands. About this time repairs were begun to the fort and Tytler had to shift his quarters to Cat Cove, only a short distance away just inside the islet called Winter Island which lay close to the Neck on the east. He was still conveniently close to the clam banks and the salt pans. He finished his pans and tended them for about a year, but with little success. 'His pans', wrote Mr Bentley, 'have not produced salt for his porridge and his medicines have not relieved him from extreme indigence.' Then in 1798 a violent storm pounded the beach with destructive waves and Tytler 'lost all his labour'.

But as usual he had already another iron in the fire. Drawing on both his medical and historical knowledge, he compiled an exhaustive *Treatise on the Plague and Yellow Fever*, containing accounts of the famous epidemics of the plague in Athens, Constantinople, London, Marseilles and Aleppo, and of the spread of yellow fever from the West Indies to North America. Towards the end of the year a subscription list for this work was opened.

Mr Bentley did not expect much of the *Treatise*. Though kindly disposed towards Tytler he had taken his measure as an author not only from his poem but from his second answer to Paine and recognized that his thoughts were unoriginal and his style a mixture of vanity and verbosity. 'He talks of himself as at least of equal rank with Paine and writes on and writes on, satisfied that he has written. . . . Men have written a *great deal*, but have not yet found out the way to write.' Though Bentley's own literary style was turgid he was well qualified to criticize others', being a man of considerable learning, a remarkable linguist, and a regular correspondent of Thomas Jefferson. Moreover he knew enough of the practices of commercial printers, no more scrupulous in Salem than in Edinburgh, to foresee that the *Treatise* would be more an exercise in bookmongering than a contribution to science. 'This', he decided, 'is an artifice of the printers, with the aid of a quack, to force a little money from the public. *Compilation*, compilation, compilation is as much the cry as *Beaucoup d'argent* from the poor Frenchmen.'

The *Treatise* ran to 568 pages when it appeared early in October 1799, and Bentley had only to dip into it to confirm his prejudice. 'If we may judge from the introduction,' he wrote, 'it is a stupid performance. . . . The style of thought is the most groveling to be imagined.' Noah Webster also attacked the book in the Salem *Gazette*, and Tytler, quick as ever to defend himself, answered back. In the course of this contest Tytler advocated a stricter enforcement of quarantine regulations in seaports. 'It is plain beyond contradiction', he wrote on 15 April 1800, 'that pestilential diseases may be introduced by means of commerce. I do not, however, mean to insinuate that commerce should be abandoned; all that I mean is to advise commercial people to take care of themselves.'

Another venture projected by Tytler in 1800 was a further exercise in 'compilation', this time doubly distilled since it was to consist of extracts from his own writings. It was to be entitled *Lectures on Diet and Regimen* and to run to two volumes, each of 360 pages. Proposals for this publication were issued by a Boston printer who had apparently been impressed by Tytler's conviction that Americans ate too much; but the work itself did not attract subscribers and never appeared.

By these and other expedients Tytler achieved with steady toil, as he had done in Scotland, a bare subsistence but no more. He was, it is clear, kindly regarded by the people of Salem and became one of the well-known 'characters' of their community. They sympathized with his troubles, respected his learning, and tolerated his eccentricities; and they did not mind his being occasionally the worse for liquor.

The twins were placed 'in good families in the town', probably as domestic servants. With their children thus provided for, Tytler and his wife managed somehow to live in their modest dwelling at Cat Cove. They did not often come into Salem and Tytler resolutely avoided becoming a member of any religious community, as he had done ever since he broke with the Glasites.

'In this retired, obscure and destitute state,' wrote Bentley after Tytler's death, 'dependant on a few friends, and with little intercourse with the world, he passed as an inoffensive man, rather pitied, than injuried, as he avoided all intercourse with the inhabitants as much as he could.' Yet the 'few friends' seem to have been respectable people. Bentley, though he did not admit him to any intimacy, was kind to him; so, it appears, was James Dalrymple, 'a highly respected and useful citizen', who had come out with the Tytlers in the *Eliza* and set up business in Salem as a watchmaker; and one who felt a really warm friendship for Tytler was young Benjamin Crowninshield, who from his early interest in science and the arts was nicknamed 'Philosopher Ben'.

Young Crowninshield was too unsophisticated to regard Tytler as critically as his elders did and he was undoubtedly one of Tytler's 'few friends' in Salem. He must often have passed along Derby Street, crossed the narrow spit of the Neck Gate with the sands on each side of it covered at every high tide, and walked over to Cat Cove to sit talking to Tytler, fascinated by the flow of his ideas on all kinds of subjects, impressed by his utopian philosophy, and specially interested by his scientific knowledge. He is the only person among those who actually knew Tytler to have left on record positive praise of his qualities. Despite Ben's youth and inexperience of the world it is clear testimony that Tytler's personality could favourably impress an intelligent mind. Ben Crowninshield became a student of William and Mary College at Williamsburg, Virginia, one of the very few to go there in those days from New England, and it was from Williamsburg, four months after Tytler's death, that he wrote to a friend this touching tribute to him:

'I believe Mr Tytler was the only man, who could balance

two ideas, and take the true difference. I believe he was the only unprejudiced philosopher, that ever wrote. His judgment, in philosophy, flowed from the fountain, but in the arts of life the stream ran muddily. If you had received from him, like me, every thing you know, your heart, like mine, would have overflowed with grief. O if he were here, the morning of my life would not be over-clouded.'

Ben returned Tytler's friendship with all the kindness that he could show him, and Mrs Tytler said later that she could not have received more from him had he been her own son. It was probably from Ben in particular that Mr Bentley acquired what he himself came to hear of Tytler's circumstances and his earlier life, for he lived with the Crowninshield family, occupying rooms in the digni-fied three-storeyed house, built in 1727, which they owned on the corner of Essex Street. Another of this family, Hannah Crownin-shield, made a watercolour sketch of Tytler which, though perhaps a posthumous likeness, is of great interest as the only authentic portrait of him apart from Kay's caricature. It explains why Bentley refers to him as 'the old man'. With white hair and a high bald forehead he has, in his late fifties, a venerable appearance worthy of the 'philosopher' Ben considered him.

In 1801 Tytler at last found regular employment, though only at a pittance. He entered into an agreement with a Salem bookseller named Barnard Bryan Macanulty, described by Mr Bentley as 'an ignorant but not very modest Irishman' and as 'very amiable, till he became addicted to intemperance'. This arrangement was for the publication of a new geography, a task well within Tytler's powers since he had performed a similar one in 1788, besides writing the article on Geography for the *Encyclopaedia Britannica*. Neither Tytler's nor Macanulty's name however inspired much confidence in the plan. Bentley, who heard of it on 13 March 1801 from Macanulty himself, commented in his diary: 'It is lamentable that so many publications in this country are evidently only catch penny pro-ductions. Not even suggested by genius, but first asked by the promise of cash for the compilation.' But when some months later Tytler was violently attacked in an Essex County newspaper for his presumption in attempting such a work, Bentley generously came to his assistance and defence. 'The invective', he wrote, 'discovered a total ignorance of the man, whatever it might conclude about his employers.'

The agreement drawn up between Tytler and Macanulty is extant (it is not, as has been thought in Salem, in Tytler's handwriting), dated 31 July 1801 and witnessed by James and John Dalrymple, the former of whom and perhaps the latter too had shared Tytler's crossing in the *Eliza*. It goes into great detail. All the work was to be Tytler's, though Macanulty engaged to provide him with any necessary books, and all the profit Macanulty's, the terms justifying Bentley's penetrating observation on Tytler's career which might indeed have applied to any part of it—'He was always careless of interest, and suffered others to profit from his labours.' Macanulty specified most comprehensively what he expected of Tytler. The *Universal Geography* was to be not only a 'just succinct and accurate' account of 'all the kingdoms and countries of and in the known world' but to cover their 'situation boundaries rivers soil natural and artificial productions curiosities manners customs history government religion laws revenue taxes naval and military strength language learning arts sciences manufactures commerce' and to include whatever matter about all these subjects might be found 'in the best and most approved works and geographies of said countries or any of them now extant'. For performing this gigantic task of research and compilation, on the scale rather of an encyclopaedia than a geography, Tytler was to receive from Macanulty remuneration at the rate of $12\frac{1}{2}$ cents for every hour's work—'the said hours to be regularly and distinctly marked down and registred by said Tytler in a book to be kept for that purpose'.

About the only liberal clause in the agreement was that specifying no time limit for the completion of the work. Tytler was to begin it 'immediately' and to finish it 'within a reasonable time'. The remuneration of $12\frac{1}{2}$ cents an hour sounds miserable, but eight hours' work a day, of which Tytler was quite capable, would mean a dollar a day which to Tytler probably seemed a satisfactory livelihood by the standards to which he had grown accustomed. He set to work and in less than a year had advanced far enough for Macanulty to issue a 16-page pamphlet of *Proposals for publishing by subscription a New System of Geography, Ancient and Modern.*

Macanulty entered into a supplementary agreement with Joseph Nancrede, the Boston bookseller, of French origin, who had projected Tytler's abortive *Lectures on Diet and Regimen.* In 1802 Nancrede sailed for Europe to procure maps for the new work. Bentley too, much against his will but from an impulse, which did him credit, to help and protect Tytler, was drawn into the scheme. Having given Tytler what encouragement he could, he felt obliged in honour 'to assist the expectations I had raised and to justify them amply to the world'. On 25 January 1802 he for the first time invited Tytler into the house on Essex Street to find out what help with the compilation he expected. Their talk rather depressed him. 'No present conjectures can be made of our success, and little honour gained from our employers', he reflected gloomily; and on 24 June, when the 'proposals' had been published, his sad reflection was 'I wish an acquaintance gave me an increasing sense of the value of the talents which Mr Tytler possesses'.

This seems to be the only extant comment on Tytler's qualifications by one who knew him and was himself a man of real learning—for Anderson's biographical sketch does not go beyond crediting him with 'a versatility of talent and a facility in writing'. Bentley's opinion confirms the impression left by Tytler's many productions that he possessed a great fund of knowledge but lacked the intellectual equipment to make much use of it. He could do a great many things but nothing very well. As a writer he was never more than a bookseller's hack, and that was all he was really fit to be.

Secure at last in steady employment at $12\frac{1}{2}$ cents an hour Tytler

7 Crowninshield House, Essex Street, Salem

8 James Tytler in 1804

worked away at the *Universal Geography* throughout 1803. He had nearly finished it by the time he reached his 58th birthday on 17 December. At the beginning of the New Year, elated perhaps by the approaching end of his drudgery, or perhaps by the return of what Burns had called 'that merry day the year begins', which must have carried his thoughts back to the traditional conviviality of his native land, he was several times noticed to be the worse for drink, though 'not generally addicted to it'.

The evening of Sunday, 8 January 1804, was cold and stormy. Snow covered the streets of Salem, driven in from the ocean by a strong east wind, and early next morning a ship about to sail for Spain with a cargo of flour dragged her anchors and was driven ashore, though without serious damage. In the course of Monday, 9 January, the snow turned to heavy rain which continued into the evening. Soon after nightfall a man named Oliver living near the Neck Gate was roused by Tytler, who had walked over from Cat Cove through the darkness and the rain to buy or borrow a candle. His errand, in mid-winter, suggests how short of common necessities he and his wife could be, but possibly the need existed only in Tytler's imagination for Oliver saw that he was very drunk—too drunk, he thought, to be wandering about in the dark in such weather with safety.

The tide was full and the shallow water covered the sands on both sides of the Neck Gate as Tytler, having got his candle, staggered away into the darkness. He never returned home. Jean waited for him all night, searched for him next morning, but told no one of his being missing, perhaps to avoid speaking of the state in which she had last seen him. She had no food in the house and at last fainted from anxiety and hunger. In the evening, as Mr Bentley recorded in his diary, 'a youth from our family went down to Tytler's to pass an hour accidentally with the old man, and found his wife senseless on the floor'. This was surely Benjamin Crowninshield. He did what he could to revive the poor woman, hurried home to raise the alarm and, while the two Tytler girls were sought out and sent to look after their mother, the Crowninshield family, Mr Bentley and their servants searched everywhere for Tytler, 'visited all his haunts and went to Marblehead', six miles away. But it was not till the Wednesday morning, 11 January, that Tytler's body was found. It was 'in the wash' on the Neck Gate's north shore, and they guessed that after leaving Oliver's he had wandered in the direction of the lights of the few houses that stood in that corner of the Neck, and so had slipped into the water which at that hour would be lapping at the sides of the Neck Gate.

The body was buried, after an inquest, the same day. News of the tragic death of the lonely old man and the ordeal of his widow had spread rapidly among the people of Salem and stirred their sympathies deeply. They crowded the East Meeting-House for the funeral service, raised on the spot a collection of 120 dollars for Mrs Tytler, and formed, as the *Register* reported next day, 'a numerous procession' to escort the coffin to its grave, with 'some of the most respected citizens' as pall-bearers.

Mr Bentley delivered a eulogy which was probably the more effective for his having had little time to prepare it, though he could speak only from his 'imperfect acquaintance' with the dead man and what he could pick up from others. In his diary that night, repeating perhaps some of the phrases he had used in public, he summed up, objectively and with remarkable insight, the mis-applied gifts, the impractical idealism, the ardour and the folly, the mixture of amiability and prickliness, toughness and weakness, that made up Tytler's ill-balanced nature. It is hard to believe that even one who had known him much better and much longer could have assessed him more fairly, even though it was not till two days later that Bentley inquired, probably of Tytler's widow, into the circumstances of his earlier life.

'It was evident', wrote Bentley on the evening of Tytler's funeral, 'he was excentric. The incidents of his life had not impaired his industry, and his thirst for universal knowledge varied too often his pursuits. He anticipated from his theory more for mankind than experience can justify our hopes to expect very soon, and he was determined by his integrity to countenance nothing which did not meet his full wishes. With the affairs of the world he was irreconcileable, and sufferings made him more unyielding and obstinate. For religion he had a love, but allied to his prejudices it could also be subject to his passions. He loved mankind, but such a world as he would not find among men. His social virtues were sincere, but more from sentiment than affection. Yet he gave unbounded confidence to those he trusted. Poverty overwhelmed him, and artificial relief gave disgrace to his exit.'

On the following Sunday Bentley recorded, 'Mrs Tytler made her first appearance in our congregation. Her husband tho' a firm Christian could not reconcile his habits to any public assembly whatever.' He offered special prayers during the service, as was his custom, for individuals who were suffering or bereaved, and included one for 'Jane Tytler' and her daughters. They were not left friendless. James Dalrymple took Jean into his house, and there is a glimpse of her a year later still lodged there, dining with a Salem doctor's family and inquiring with earnest affection after Ben Crowninshield who was then in Williamsburg.

A year later Jean was attempting to earn a living from what she could remember of her husband's practice, and advertising in the *Register* that she could prepare 'ether, dulcified spirits of nitre, spirits of vitriol and essence of peppermint' and other medicines for the medical profession. But this venture did not support her and she at length took refuge in the almshouse built just inside the Neck only a short distance from the scene of Tytler's death. By a strange irony she was later joined there by Barnard Macanulty whose business had collapsed.

Jean lived on to the age of 84, respected as the widow of 'Dr James Tytler' and 'a very worthy woman', and died in the almshouse on 2 January 1834. Of her daughters one at least married and

147

had a family, for it was a granddaughter of Tytler's, a Mrs Allen, who presented to the Essex Institute in Salem the copy which it possesses of his *Treatise on the Plague and Yellow Fever*. In Massachusetts as in Scotland there may still be living today some descendants of Balloon Tytler.

Appendix

Indictment of James Tytler

GEORGE, &c. WHEREAS it is humbly meant and complained to us by our right trusty ROBERT DUNDAS, Esq; of Arniston, our Advocate, for our interest, upon JAMES TYTLER, chemist, residing in King's Park, in the neighbourhood of Edinburgh, and in the county of Edinburgh: THAT ALBEIT, by the laws of this and all other well governed realms, the wickedly and feloniously writing or printing, or causing to be written or printed, any seditious libel or writing; AS ALSO, the wickedly and feloniously distributing and circulating any such seditious writing, or libel, when so printed; OR the causing the same to be distributed and circulated among the inhabitants of a populous city, the metropolis of a country, are crimes of an heinous nature, dangerous to the public peace, and severely punishable: YET TRUE IT IS, AND OF VERITY, That he the said James Tytler has presumed to commit, and is guilty of all and each, or one or other, of the foresaid crimes, actor, or art and part: IN SO FAR AS, upon one or other of the days of the month of November in this present year, to the Public Prosecutor unknown, the said James Tytler did, in the county of Edinburgh, or at some other place to the Public Prosecutor unknown, wickedly and feloniously compose and write, or cause to be composed or written, a seditious libel or writing, addressed 'To the people and their friends,' whereof the tenor follows:

'To the PEOPLE and their FRIENDS
'A REFORM in Parliament being now universally talked of, it

seems necessary for you to consider of the means by which that reform is to be accomplished, which means have not yet been seriously taken into consideration by any person, or number of persons, that I have heard of. It is said, that Mr Pitt will perhaps bring in a reform; and I understand that this has been held forth to you by certain Colonels and Captains, (perhaps I may mistake their titles) in whom I wish you to put no confidence. What right has Mr Pitt to make the Parliament good or bad as he pleases? Or what right have the Parliament to lengthen or shorten the time of their own sitting? Will you still suffer yourselves to be duped, and to be made the tools of every one who thinks proper to assume the authority over you? I have been told, that those who would be your leaders, advise you to petition Parliament. The proposal involves itself in contradiction. The Parliament has already showed [*sic*] itself unworthy of confidence, and it has usurped a power to which it has no right. If the House of Commons is composed of the *representatives* of the people, these must be the servants of the people. Will you then be so absurd as to petition your own servants, or people who ought to be so? But the truth is, that the Members of this House have become the masters not only of the people, but of the King also. How many petitions have of late been presented to the House of Commons, and how few to the King? As the Popish priests absorbed the worship due to the Deity by stocks and stones and rascally saints, so have the House of Commons artfully drawn away the attention of the people of Britain from the King to themselves. Those who advise you to petition the House of Commons, insidiously and slily tell you, that these are your only just and lawful masters; yet those very persons will rail against the corruptions of the House of Commons as much as any body; nay, they are part of the House whom they desire you to petition; so that their advice ends in the very modest request, that you would petition themselves! But, besides this absurdity, you must consider the House of Commons as your enemies. They affect to consider themselves as the *democratical* part of the constitution. They are not; they are a vile junto of aristocrats. The majority of them are landholders; and every landholder is a despot, in the most true and literal sense of the word. He can, directly or indirectly, extort from the country what he pleases: He can raise the price of provisions; he can turn people out of their possessions; he can drive them to the utmost ends of the earth; and, in short, turn the country, at least that part of it which he possesses, into a wilderness, if he pleases. It is this monstrous power of the landholders that you have to combat; and it is the want of something to balance this power, that is the true foundation of all the grievances you labour under. If you wish a remedy for the evils which you suffer, and are resolved to petition, surely you must petition the person who has it in his power to grant the remedy; and this is no other than the King, whom you seem entirely to have forgot. You cannot be ignorant that the King can dissolve Parliament, and call them together when he pleases. If you wish Parliament to sit only three years, petition the King to dissolve it at that term; and, if he consents, you have your desire, at the same time that the Parliament has no reason to complain. If you wish to have an equal representation, let those who are not represented petition the King; let them set forth, that they are oppressed and enslaved by an assembly of aristocrats, who call themselves the representatives of the people, but are not; let them request that the King will allow them to choose representatives for themselves; and that they may choose any person of good understanding and character to this office, though he should not be a landholder; nay, let them make an exception, that these representatives shall not be landholders, and it will be so much the better. Let not the minister, or his *spies*, however, deceive you, by promising a reform, and admitting the inferior class of landholders as electors, or capable of being elected, as I am told he has offered. Thus you would be overwhelmed with an inundation of tyrants, and in a worse situation than you are. Let not money, or land, or houses, be thought to make a man fit for being an elector or representative; an honest and upright behaviour is the only qualification. Wealth has too long usurped the place and the rights of virtue;

let virtue now resume its own power and dignity, to the exclusion of every thing else. Remember, that it was by an unwarrantable stretch of power, that the Commons enlarged the duration of their own sitting. If they get this power sanctified by a petition from the National Convention, it is precisely what they want; and instead of obtaining any reform, the chains of the nation will be rivetted.'

Which seditious libel or writing the said James Tytler delivered to William Turnbull printer in Edinburgh, upon one or other of the days of the said month of October, in this present year, or of the month of November following, and employed him to print the same; and he having accordingly done so, and thrown off five hundred copies, or thereby, thereof, which were delivered by him to the said James Tytler, on the 26th day of the said month of November, or some one or other of the days of that month, or of October preceding, or of December following, he the said James Tytler did, immediately thereafter, and upon one or other of the days of the said months, wickedly and feloniously distribute and circulate, or cause to be distributed and circulated, amongst the inhabitants of the city of Edinburgh and its suburbs, a considerable number of the said seditious libel or writing, so printed, as aforesaid, to the amount of two hundred and fifty, or thereby: And the said James Tytler, with the view, and for the purpose of inflaming still more the minds of the inhabitants of the said city of Edinburgh and its suburbs, inciting them to break the public peace, and of inspiring them with sentiments hostile to our happy constitution, and injurious to the peace and happiness of the inhabitants of this realm, did, within some few days after the so printing, publishing, and distributing and circulating of the said seditious libel, as aforesaid, compose and write, or cause to be composed and written, a wicked and seditious paragraph, of the following tenor:

'If the King do not hear you, our Magna Charta hath this for its basis, that the people need not pay any contributions towards the public exigencies of that country to which they do not belong; for it bears, that we must appear, either in person, or by our representatives, and calmly and deliberately put our hand, as it were, to our pocket, and pay what we please, or what is agreed to; and as this at present is not the case, but only with a small number, the rest of the nation are either slaves, or not of their community; and consequently not under their law, until such time, so to speak, as we be naturalized. This is the law of our Magna Charta: And as we are without the national bond, in this we are beyond their law, as by it we must have our voice in framing our laws, or they are none of ours; consequently, we may as timidly submit to laws imposed on us by the Pope, as submit to laws imposed on us by such a junto. The conclusion is, if the King hear you not, keep your money in your pockets, and frame your own laws, and the minority must submit to the majority.'

Which seditious writing or paragraph the said James Tytler did . . . also deliver to the said William Turnbull with directions to print the same on the back or second page of the aforesaid wicked and seditious libel; for which purpose the said James Tytler returned to the said William Turnbull such of the copies of the said seditious libel . . . as had not before that time been distributed . . . to the number of two hundred and fifty, or thereby; and the said William Turnbull having accordingly, in terms of the said directions, printed . . . the said . . . paragraph, on the back of the copies of the aforesaid seditious libel . . . he did thereafter deliver the whole of the same, or nearly so, to the said James Tytler: And he the said James Tytler did thereafter . . . distribute and circulate . . . the said seditious libel, originally printed and thrown off as aforesaid, with the addition of the said seditious paragraph as printed on the said second page of the same. And the said James Tytler having been apprehended on suspicion of being guilty of the said crimes, and carried before John Pringle, Esq; Sheriff-depute of the county of Edinburgh, he did in his presence emit and sign a declaration upon the 4th day of December 1792, which was likewise subscribed by the said John Pringle; and being to be used in evidence against the said James Tytler at his trial, will . . . be lodged in due time with the

Clerk of the High Court of Justiciary [with copies of the first and second impressions of the seditious libel], before which the said James Tytler is to be tried, that he may have an opportunity of seeing the same. . . . The said James Tytler OUGHT to be punished with the pains of law, to deter others from committing the like crimes in all time coming. OUR WILL IS, &c.—

National Library of Scotland L.C. 1133(4).
The original is unparagraphed.

Bibliography

BOOKS

[Robert Meek:] *Biographical Sketch of the Life of James Tytler*, 1805.

R. H. Cromek: *Reliques of Robert Burns*, 1808.

R. H. Cromek: *Select Scotish Songs*, 1810.

Original Portraits . . . by the late John Kay, 1877.

Bibliotheca Britannica.

Robert Chambers: *Biographical Dictionary of Eminent Scotsmen*, 1847.

Robert Chambers: *The Songs of Scotland prior to Burns*, 1862.

Robert Chambers: *Traditions of Edinburgh*, 1825.

Hugo Arnot: *The History of Edinburgh*, 1779.

A. J. Youngson: *The Making of Classical Edinburgh*, 1966.

Charles A. Malcolm: *Holyrood*, 1937.

Peter Halkerston: *A Treatise on the Sanctuary of Holyroodhouse*, 1831.

[Edward Topham:] *Letters from Edinburgh written in the years 1774 and 1775*, 1776.

W. J. Couper: *The Edinburgh Periodical Press*, 1908.

Henry Cockburn: *Memorials of his Time*, 1856.

Henry Cockburn: *The Journal of Henry Cockburn*, 1874.

Robert Kerr: *Memoirs of the Life, Writings, and Correspondence of William Smellie*, 1811.

Harold W. Thompson (ed.): *The Anecdotes and Egotisms of Henry Mackenzie*, 1927.

James Fergusson (ed.): *Letters of George Dempster to Sir Adam Fergusson, 1756–1813*, 1934.

Alistair and Henrietta Tayler: *Lord Fife and his Factor*, 1925.

Hans Hecht: *Robert Burns*, 1936.

J. De Lancey Ferguson (ed.): *The Letters of Robert Burns*, 1931.

William Stenhouse: *Illustrations of the Lyric Poetry and Music of Scotland*, 1853.

J. F. Hodgson: *The History of Aeronautics in Great Britain*, 1924.

Vincent Lunardi: *An Account of Five Aerial Voyages in Scotland*, 1786.

H. W. Meikle: *Scotland and the French Revolution*, 1912.

G. W. T. Omond: *The Lord Advocates of Scotland*, 1883.

Holden Furber: *Henry Dundas*, 1931.

Autobiography of Mrs Fletcher, 1875.

Harriet S. Tapley: *Salem Imprints*, 1768–1825.

Diary of William Bentley, D.D., Massachusetts Historical Society, 1905–14.

Essex Institute Historical Collections.

PERIODICALS

The Scots Magazine.
The Gentleman's Magazine.
The Bee.
Caledonian Mercury.
Edinburgh Advertiser.
Edinburgh Evening Courant.
Scottish Historical Review, vii.
Book of the Old Edinburgh Club, xix.
Burns Chronicle, 1925.
Salem Gazette.
Salem Register.
William and Mary College Quarterly, second series, xi.

MANUSCRIPTS

Exchequer Records: *Bounties paid to whaling ships.* Scottish Record Office: E 508/62–74.

Divorce process in the Commissary Court of Edinburgh: Elizabeth Rattray against James Tytler. S.R.O. CC 8/5/19; CC 8/6/50; CC 8/7/34.

Register of Protections by the Bailie of Holyrood (photostat). S.R.O. RH 2/8/17.

Process, Rattray or Tytler against Ballantyne and others. S.R.O. Midlothian Sheriff Court Records.

Squib on balloon ascents. Edinburgh University Library: Dc. 6. 111, f. 38.

Tytler's letters to Anderson. National Library of Scotland: Adv. MSS. 22.4.11, ff. 38–9.

Home Office correspondence. Public Record Office: H.O. 102/6 and 102/7 (photostats in S.R.O.).

Indictment of James Tytler in the Court of Justiciary. Nat. Lib. Scot. L.C. 1133(4).

Index